God's Sayings

Proverbs, Enigmas & Riddles

To know wisdom and instruction;
to understand a proverb, an
enigma and the riddles of the wise.

Proverbs 1:2, 6

Randy & Barbara Walter

God's Sayings: Proverbs, Enigmas & Riddles

Berlin, Maryland, USA
ISBN **978-0-9890789-9-3**
Published by Shiloh Publishing in March, 2021

Printed in the United States of America.

Contents

SHILOH MINISTRIES BOOKS

LET'S GET FREE: *Rightly Dividing The Word Of Truth*

There are things we each need to be freed from. Religious spirits masquerade as Christianity but actually separate us from God by trapping us in legalism, tradition, superstition and fear. **LET'S GET FREE** exposes hidden religious spirits and shows how to be free.

$15 each *(includes shipping)*

MARRIAGE GOD'S WAY

God rescued our marriage by teaching us *The Mirror Image Principle*: "Your relationship with your spouse is a mirror image of your relationship with Me." This book is filled with things the Lord told us on how to strengthen marriage and faith.

$12 each *(includes shipping)*

Name Your Gates & Take Back Your Cities

Applying these God-given tools is helping people transform cities and take territory.

$12 each *(includes shipping)*

Things Hoped For Prayers & Declarations

Companion booklet for *Name Your Gates & Take Back Your Cities*. Encouraging and effective prayers, organized by topics. Easy to carry with you and use.

$10 each *(includes shipping)*

Send check and mailing address to: **Shiloh Ministries • 209 West St. Berlin, Maryland 21811** • ThingsHopedFor@comcast.net

MAKE THEM REMEMBER YOUR NAME

The inspirational life of Lt. Col. Kenny Cox (USA Ret.), who was decorated for valor after rescuing many people at the Pentagon on 9/11.

$12 each *(includes shipping)*

Things Hoped For

25 years of prophetic wisdom – Barbara's stories and adventures, Randy's teachings and revelations. Readers call it *"an honest portrayal of the walk of faith"* • *"the most profoundly faith-building book I ever read"* • *"delightfully refreshing, enlightening, and very sobering."*

$15 each *(includes shipping)*

Where Do You Hurt? Where Do You Hide? *The Rehearsal*

These books free people from fear and shame to walk in God's destiny for their lives.

$10 apiece • $15 for both *(includes shipping)*

Make Room for Joy

The latest booklet in our *Timeless Wisdom* series.

$5 each *(includes shipping)*

Timeless Wisdom

Powerful messages from the Lord on *Kingdom Living*, *Prosperous Living* and *Revival Living*.

Set of 3 for $10 *(includes shipping)*

Dedication

God's Sayings: Proverbs, Enigmas & Riddles is dedicated to the memory of my dear wife, Barbara, who went to be with the Lord on May 17, 2020. We had completed about one-third of this book when she became too ill to continue. Some chapters are in her voice and sound like she is still with us.

Barbara was the love of my life, my best friend and my constant companion. It was she who led me to the Lord in 1982. In many ways she was my mentor and not just my partner. Knowledgeable and discerning, she knew how to get to the root of a matter. That is why so many people sought her advice as a spiritual mother.

Through this book, the chapters she wrote keep her alive for we who knew her. And they will make her alive to those who didn't. So I dedicate this last book we wrote together to her memory and to the glory of God.

Randy Walter

1

Don't make plans until you know the rules.

"Do not boast about tomorrow, for you do not know what a day may bring forth" (Proverbs 27:1 NKJV).

By Randy

Barbara and I love making plans and filling out to-do lists. So when the Lord told us, **"Don't make plans until you know the rules,"** we didn't understand. We believed the discipline of planning to be good stewardship and a wise use of time.

The more we discussed it, the more we gained insight. This principle has to do not only with completing daily chores but our long-range aspirations, even our ministry vision.

We viewed what the Lord told us in light of Proverbs 29:18 (KJV), **"Where there is no vision, the people perish…"** The Lord was not telling us to abandon our vision for the future. He was saying to check with Him for the details of accomplishing it.

We repeated what the Lord said over and over to each other: **"Don't make plans until you know the rules."** Then the Lord explained, **"'Until you know the rules' means 'until you see what I AM doing.'"**

We must wait until He reveals to us what He is doing. It is not only futile but arrogant to believe we can second-guess Him without first inquiring to see what He requires of us.

The Bible tells us that in our own understanding, we cannot anticipate God. In Isaiah 55:9 (KJV), He declares, **"For as the heavens are higher than the earth, so are My ways higher than your ways, and My thoughts than your thoughts."**

Proverbs 20:24 is more specific about our ability to make plans on our own: **"A man's steps are of the Lord; how then can a man understand his own way?"** (NKJV).

We try to practice this principle every day. In the morning when we talk about what we want to accomplish, we remind each other, "We don't know God's rules yet."

This goes along with when He told us to be

"Alert, Flexible and Available."

1

When Barbara and I are available to God, He sends us people during the day who come for ministry. They might need prayer, counseling or just fellowship. We often have many people come at different times throughout the week. Sometimes we don't get to our chores or activities. God makes the rules.

The Lord taught us to pray that He regulate our schedule. This gives us peace, knowing whoever He sends is His plan for us.

"There are many plans in a man's heart, nevertheless the Lord's counsel – that will stand" (Proverbs 19:21 NKJV).

At a ministry retreat many years ago, one of the speakers related how his young daughter would interrupt him while he was preparing his Sunday sermon. The household understood that this was when Daddy needed to be by himself, but the girl continued to demand his attention.

Trying not to get annoyed, he was finally able to make her happy. Then he asked the Lord how to have a right attitude. The response he heard was, **"The ministry is in the interruptions."** We never know when an unplanned moment or an off-the-cuff comment man be exactly what someone needs.

There were days when Barbara and I met with one person after another from morning until night, and we had joy knowing the Lord had sent each one. But there are also those who are time-wasters. The Lord once said to us, **"A person who wastes a lot of time will waste a lot of your time too."**

When we yield to God's rules rather than cling to our own plans, then we have peace. This principle has made us more flexible and less agitated when we don't get to do what we hoped to get done in a day.

"A man's heart plans his way, but the Lord directs his steps" (Proverbs 16:9 NKJV).

God reminds us often that He has our best interest at heart. It's all about trusting Him. He sees the whole picture while we see only our little part of it. He arranges everything for everyone's well-being, and sometimes that means what is important to us at the moment has to wait until the other pieces are in place.

2

You can't find the new season in the old model.

"Therefore, purge out the old leaven, that you may be a new lump" (I Corinthians 5:7 NKJV).

God's Sayings – *Proverbs, Enigmas & Riddles*

By Randy

A couple we had not seen in many years called us out of the blue, and we invited them over for dinner. As we ate, the wife confided that they were discontent because they didn't know of a church that was a "fit" for them.

They like being active in a congregation, and they want to be part of the move of God. She said they felt left out because they couldn't find a church that embraces what they believe God is currently doing.

I told her what I heard the Lord say: **"She's looking for the new season in the old model."**

This is a new season. We cannot fully enter it as long as we are still tied to the old season. It is possible to enter our new season but not be engaged in it.

As the Hebrew children left Egypt, they entered a new season. When they whined and complained, they were still attached to the old season rather than committed to the new one. If they had engaged in the new season, they never would have reverted to the idol worship of Egypt.

As most marriages do, ours has gone through many seasons. Barbara went from doing a puppet and drama ministry with her children at the beginning, to ministering with me. We started producing a regional newspaper for a Christian radio station. Then God called Barbara into a feeding outreach in nearby Ocean City. We helped each other with our diverse activities.

Our kids were growing, so Barbara's puppet shows and children's church ministry ended. After 27 years of our doing the newspaper, the Christian radio station went out of business. So we transitioned into a new season of writing books and using our house as a place for ministry meetings.

We started leading prayer journeys and raising up intercessors, while hosting speakers to teach and minister. Then the Lord had us begin teaching on writing. Many times these activities overlapped. Each one came with its own revelations. God's seasons are like the weather. It can be Indian summer at the same time it's actually fall. Or you can have snow in the spring.

Whenever we were doing new things at the same time as we did old ones,

2

the former things quickly fell away to make room for the new. Although we once reached tens of thousands of readers each month through the newspaper, we believe what we do now engages people on a deeper level. We mentor and teach them to pray, write, and help them discover their spiritual gifts. Our ceiling has become their floor. Some have gone way beyond us. Those we have taught now do greater things – more and better – than we ever did.

The Bible says the latter days of the righteous will be greater. **"They shall still bear fruit in old age; they shall be fresh and flourishing"** (Psalm 92:14 NKJV). It's like the latter temple whose glory was greater than the former (Haggai 2:9).

To consider us "retired" is not really accurate. We asked the Lord about the Western concept of retirement and He said:

"The evil of retirement is that it carries with it a sense of entitlement. Many retired people are so concerned about what they earned that life becomes all about them."

When we first started Shiloh Ministries, we thought we needed a director, and hired a woman who raised eyebrows among our friends. But we went by what the Lord told us years earlier when we were building our house. Every time we came to the construction site, the carpenters were sitting on their tailgate drinking coffee. "Trust who I send you," the Lord said so we would not get upset. We assumed His words still applied.

When people said, "Are you *sure*?" about our ministry director, we went by what the Lord said before. We didn't realize that we were trying to apply an old model in a new season.

Hiring a director turned out to be a huge mistake. Three months and many thousands of dollars later, she flew the coop and there was nothing to show for it except major embarrassment.

When we asked the Lord to explain why "Trust who I send you" did not work when we applied it again, He reminded us of the old saying—

"That was then; this is now."

3

A person who takes offense easily gives offense readily.

"Love... does not behave rudely, does not seek its own, is not provoked... bears all things, believes all things, hopes all things, endures all things"

(1 Corinthians 13:4-7 NKJV).

God's Sayings – *Proverbs, Enigmas & Riddles*

By Barbara

When the Lord instructed us to pray the Lord's Prayer differently, He changed everything. We had been repeating it the same way we learned it as children. Instead, He taught us to say: **"Give us this day our daily bread, and forgive us our *offenses* as we forgive those who *offend* us."**

Substituting the word "offenses" for the word "trespasses" made it much more personal and convicting. It caused us to realize that whenever we give offense, we were ultimately offending God, who sent Jesus to die for each person we offend or take offense at.

The Good News Translation of the Lord's Prayer in Matthew 6 says, **"Forgive us the wrongs we have done, as we forgive the wrongs that others have done to us."** We are only forgiven to the extent that we forgive those we blame.

We stopped to think about how easily we can take offense, and how offensive we can be in return. Proverbs 19:11 (ESV) says, **"Good sense makes one slow to anger, and it is his glory to overlook an offense."**

Randy used to take offense at people's driving and say things like, "They're all out to get me." He had to learn to pray against imagined offense.

The Lord pointed out to him that every time he grumbled, complained or cursed someone else for their driving, the curse boomeranged back on him. Those people weren't even thinking about him. It was arrogant and selfish of him not to pray for their safety and well-being.

To help us focus on how we respond to others, the Lord explained:

"A person who takes offense easily gives offense readily.

"When you take offense, you take people hostage. That's when you give in to the sin of manipulation.

"Just because you were provoked, is it someone else's fault? If this is how you react to a small difference, how will you respond to persecution?

"When you forgive, don't just give it lip service. 'Forgive' means to give up your right to be offended, and rejoin your unity without hesitation.

"If you say you forgive and retain offense, you are still holding a hostage. Any residue of anger is an attempt to control.

3

"When you forgive, you don't just give up the right to be angry; you give up the right to dwell on what you were angry about.

"Unity cannot exist where there is offense. Offense cannot take place when people give up their right to be offended. That's the fruit of humbling yourselves.

"Unity revolves around humility. It's the grace I give to the humble.

"Absence of unity and humility are the sticks in the beaver's dam that stop up the river of blessing."

Jesus views offense very differently than we do. He told us:

"It denies My attributes of righteousness and holiness to say I'm not offended by sin. But My offense and man's offense are very different. Man is offended at sin out of self-righteousness, because he wants to prove himself by his works. I AM offended at sin out of love for the sinner, within the context of ultimate, infinite mercy."

The Lord gave us six basic rules for letting go of an offense:

"One. It's the other person's problem. It's not your problem unless you make it your problem.

"Two. Even though it sounds personal, don't take it personally.

"Three. Don't add to the problem by prolonging it. If someone unloads on you, the more you say, the more the other person has to take issue with, and the longer it takes to get past it.

"Four. Remember that the other person is not the source of your peace. Therefore, he can't take it from you unless you give it to him.

"Five. When you are insulted and your character is impugned and your efforts at reconciliation are rejected, think of your crucifixion as mostly painless. Be glad that's all you have to suffer for the sake of your beliefs.

"Six. When you learn not to interpret transgressions as personal, you will walk in forgiveness. It is not really the other person that transgresses against you. It is a spirit which wants to put him in bondage – and you, too, if you let it."

4

The solution comes wrapped up in the problem, and it's going to take work.

"And Moses said to the people, 'Do not be afraid. Stand still, and see the salvation of the Lord, which He will accomplish for you today. For the Egyptians whom you see today, you shall see again no more forever'" (Exodus 14:13 NKJV).

God's Sayings – *Proverbs, Enigmas & Riddles*

By Randy

In the biblical account of the Exodus, the Hebrew people believed they were pinned against the Red Sea by Pharaoh's army, with no way of escape. The waters appeared to be the problem, but in reality they were God's solution. The people went through the sea on dry land, then the waters returned to cover every last soldier, horse and chariot.

The work of faith was to traverse the sea. The word "Hebrew" can be traced to a root word meaning "to pass over."

When the Lord told us, **"The solution comes wrapped up in the problem, and it's going to take work,"** it took us about a week to receive the revelation.

It was new to me because I always thought the problem arrived first, then it was necessary to search for the solution until you found it. The Lord was saying that they both arrive together, and we can choose to look at the problem, or look past it for the solution.

Now problems are exciting because we know we're going to learn some life principles from them, plus receive the benefit of a wonderful solution. Sometimes solutions are witty inventions, which we also pray for.

"I wisdom dwell with prudence, and find out knowledge of witty inventions" (Proverbs 8:12 KJV). It only reads like this in the King James Version. In most other translations it goes, **"I, wisdom, dwell with prudence, and find out knowledge and discretion."** But we first learned this verse in the King James, so we pray for witty inventions.

We live on the second floor of our house. Whenever it was time to empty the trash, I had to go down a flight of steps to the trash can outdoors. Our town has provided residents with large capacity trash cans with wheels and hinged lids. The Lord showed us to fasten an eye hook to the lid, attach a rope to it with the clasp from a dog's leash, and run the rope up to our second story deck. Now, rather than running up and down a flight of steps, I just pull the rope from upstairs to open the lid, and drop in our trash bags. It's fun. We call them "air drops." It is a witty invention.

Witty inventions are not just given to us. Our wood stove is also on the second floor. That means lugging heavy firewood up a flight of stairs. After one winter of twisting my back so we could keep warm, I asked a friend with a welding shop if he could make a mechanism that would bring up the wood with less effort so I would not injure myself.

Our friend devised a small crane which uses a boat trailer winch to crank slings of wood up to our second floor deck. It is a witty invention that I still use 30 years later.

Barbara was having sciatica problems. One morning she lost the strength in her upper legs and couldn't get off the toilet. She said, "God, I can't get up." He showed her how to get off and said, **"Get a taller toilet."**

Barbara gets out of bed first in the morning. By the time I got downstairs, she had already researched a taller toilet and a bidet toilet seat. That very day we ordered the seat and I bought the toilet from our local home improvement store. Also the same day we got a check in the mail for $300 from a couple we had only met once, and who knew nothing about our needs. That covered the cost of everything.

We were going to have a home meeting so we didn't have time to install the toilet. After the meeting ended, two of our guests told us they wanted to put it in and it would only take a half-hour. And that's exactly what happened.

We had a problem. The Lord gave us the solution. He sent the money we needed, then provided the manpower to install it. Voilà! Just like that, it all fell into place. God is good.

Once He told us, **"The answer to every question and the solution to every problem can be found through wisdom and humility."** Wisdom and humility mean not to worry but to experience the peace that comes from trusting God.

Barbara likes to repeat an old folk fable (parable) about a mule that fell down a well. The farmer who owned him knew he couldn't get him out and he would die, so he began to shovel dirt over the mule in the well.

The mule shook every load of dirt off his back and took a step up. He continued to do this until he was able to walk right out of the well.

The solution came wrapped up in the problem; it just took work to get rid of the dirt.

5

Teach me what I need to know and help me understand.

"Teach me Your ways, O Lord;
make them known to me"
(Psalm 25:4 GNT).

By Randy

God is always talking to us, teaching us. Everyone can hear Him, but not everyone recognizes the various ways He communicates. People pray and often don't expect God to speak back to them.

When Barbara and I went on an out-of-town trip early in our marriage, I was tired and wanted to veg out – go on autopilot. As a creative person, she was inspired by our surroundings and started getting ideas for artistic projects. She was excited as she talked about them, but all I could hear was work being made for me, and I wanted a break. So I stopped having fun. I stopped engaging.

By the time we got back go our hotel room, Barbara could see I was shutting down, so she asked me to pray. I groaned on and on to the Lord about how hard she worked. I listed every negative reason why she shouldn't do what she was planning, but it was really that I didn't want anything required of me.

When I finished "praying," she glared angrily at me and said, "That wasn't a prayer to God, that was a lecture to me. Now you'd better *really* pray! And don't open your mouth!"

I closed my eyes to escape the tension in the room, and silently asked God what I had done wrong. I paused, not expecting a response, and heard these words: **"All she wants to do is praise Me with her gifts, and you won't let her. The reason you don't trust her is you don't trust Me."**

My eyes popped open and I told her what happened. Both of us were amazed. The Lord replied to a prayer and made it a dialogue. "That was God!" Barbara declared. We learned that we could hear Him, and that He wanted to have a deeper relationship with us – a two-way exchange. Our entire life together was altered in a moment. Later, the Lord taught us to pray, **"Teach me what I need to know and help me understand."**

Not long afterward, Barbara wanted to repaint the exterior of our old house. She asked me to select the colors. Big mistake. She is the artist. She knows what colors go together and look best. I don't.

I picked what appealed to me – gaudy gold for the exterior and a dark chocolate for the shutters and trim. She hated it. The kids hated it. Everyone hated it. They said it looked like a hot dog slathered with mustard.

Barbara was honoring me by letting me choose. Her intentions were better than my judgment. Through that and other experiences, the Lord taught us, **"Yield to the one who has the gift."** So it's not a matter of someone being in charge; instead it's about the wisdom of humility.

Many years later as we were building our new house, I had learned not to assert my taste in areas where I'm not gifted. When Barbara asked what color to paint one of the rooms, this time I replied, "I really don't have a preference. I'd like you to choose." I wasn't being passive. I was surrendering the right to an opinion so we could take advantage of her gift.

Our life became a reflection of Amos 3:3 (NKJV), **"Can two walk together, unless they are agreed?"** We were becoming a team.

A lot of people envy the gifts they see in others. The opposite is when we deny our own gifts, usually due to fear of rejection. Denying one's gift is false humility. It disrespects the sovereignty of God, who gave us our gifts and made is stewards over them.

"God has not given us a spirit of fear, but of power and of love and of a sound mind" (II Timothy 1:7 NKJV).

When we don't understand something, it can create fear. At the beginning of our marriage, Barbara and I feared many things – credit cards, computers, the Internet, cell phones, technology in general. So we failed to utilize convenient and beneficial ministry tools because of our fears.

I was even afraid to let Barbara write because she had no training. But she does not learn in classroom settings; she learns from watching. By observing me, she developed the ability to do what I did. Now she is my editor. and we write everything together. Sometimes it's hard for people to figure out where one of us stops and the other begins. We even put words in each others' mouths.

The Lord told us, "Everyone has a special ministry for which he has been created. I don't use pinch-hitters. People are not waiting in line to do your assignment. So why would you doubt that I will help you accomplish what I made you for?

"Heaven and Earth are waiting for your ministry. Angels are tuning their ears to hear you glorify Me. People are dying to hear you praise Me."

6

Gratitude creates an atmosphere for increase.

"From them will come thanksgiving and the sound of people celebrating. I will increase them; they will not be decreased; I will honor them; they will not be despised" (Jeremiah 30:19 CJB).

By Barbara

Of all *God's Sayings* we have learned, this is the one we repeated to each other more than any other:

"Gratitude creates an atmosphere for increase."

We said it so much that our grandchildren even learned it. Whenever we tell it, people's faces light up. It is a sweeping revelation.

We had long held to the standby in I Timothy 6:6, **"Now godliness with contentment is great gain"** (NKJV). But this new statement put it in a different light, and it has become a cornerstone in our lives.

Not that we were looking for ways to get more; however, increase comes automatically when you're grateful. As you become grateful in one area, it permeates every part of your thinking and sparks the realization of how much we all have to be grateful for.

The Psalms are filled with gratitude to God **"who daily loads us with benefits"** (Psalm 68:19 NKJV). After all, what do we have that we haven't been given? It's in Him that we live and move and have our being (Acts 17:28).

Gratitude is recognizing God as our source; and when we thank Him for His love and grace and faithfulness to us, we feel closer to Him. That is our reward. Matthew 6:33 tells us that when we seek Him first, everything we need is supplied.

When a couple came to us for prayer many years ago, the Lord gave us this message for them that applies to us all:

"Don't compare. Whenever you compare, you become dissatisfied and unhappy, because comparing leads to envy and it blocks faith.

"When you are grateful, it's because you have your eyes on Me. Regardless of how you pray and what you expect, whatever I give you will always be enough when you are grateful.

"There is no joy in comparing but there is ultimate joy when you are grateful. Being grateful isn't so hard; it comes from trusting Me. Once you make up your mind to trust Me, then being grateful is easy.

"Once you're of a mind to be grateful, if you try to list all the things you're grateful for, you could never do it. It puts you in a totally different mind-set.

"Likewise, when you compare and envy, that puts you in a mind-set where no matter what you have, it's never enough. So this is My word to My children for this hour: Be grateful and don't compare."

Here is the entire message the Lord originally gave us about gratitude:

"Gratitude creates an atmosphere for increase. Being grateful for everything is the key. Look at all of the traps gratitude helps you avoid: Self-pity, entitlement, resentment, greed, lust and anger are a few. See what a great strategy gratitude is?

"Properly practiced, gratitude helps you avoid disappointment and indignation. As an active strategy for wellness, it promotes healing. It balances the three parts of your being because it is an act of worship. It leaves little room for fear.

"Gratitude and contentment are the same thing. They enhance godliness as you set your affection on things above and not things below. That is great gain."

About four months after he told us that, Randy was listening to an interview on secular radio in which someone gave a corollary to what God told us. The interviewee remarked, "Ingratitude invites a spirit of poverty."

Gratitude is the theme of the popular Christian song "Give Thanks." In his lyrics, Don Moen wrote:

> Give thanks with a grateful heart.
> Give thanks to the Holy One.
> Give thanks because He's given Jesus Christ, His Son.
> And now let the weak say, "I am strong."
> Let the poor say, "I am rich. Because of what the Lord has done for us."

"He who did not spare His own Son, but delivered Him up for us all, how shall He not with Him also freely give us all things?" (Romans 8:32 NKJV).

That is an atmosphere for increase.

7

What you honor, honors you.

"By humility and the fear of the Lord are riches and honor and life" (Proverbs 22:4 NKJV).

By Randy

One morning while I was taking a shower, the Lord showed me to convene our home meetings by assigning places of honor to His attributes. It reflected the ancient custom of reserving the best seats at feasts for the most esteemed guests. Then the Lord started listing the aspects of His nature we should honor. Now we open our meetings with this prayer:

We assign places of honor to: God's Sovereign Glory; Healing, Deliverance and Encouragement; Revelation and Praise; the Love and Peace of God; God's Government; the Joy of God's Salvation; Signs, Miracles and Wonders; Prophecy and Worship; Holiness, Faith and Repentance.

We've seen all these things manifest in our home. As we have assigned them places of honor, they have honored us with their presence. Our guests, whether attending a meeting or coming for a visit, comment that they sense God's peace, presence and love on our property.

The Lord told us, "What you honor, honors you."

Thirty years ago, just after we finished building our house and moved in, we prayed in each room and asked God what to name them. We had been calling the living room the Grand Room because of its vaulted ceiling. The Lord told us instead to "call it the Great Room because in this room I will reveal My greatness." And He has.

We do our morning and evening devotions together in the Great Room. That is where the Lord speaks to us most of the time. There we receive revelation and learn more about Him. Our home meetings are held in this room. We have witnessed healings and deliverances, and seen people encouraged by prophetic words from the Lord.

Many guest speakers have told us they enjoy ministering in our house because it's so easy to prophesy here. That's because we honor prophecy.

We also honor rest. In the morning, part of our devotions is resting in the Lord. This did not come naturally to us because we both were workaholics. Every day, we put on soaking music and sit before the Lord. The Lord gave us this prayer for our soaking times, which we pray each morning:

"I commit my being to the grace and authority of the Almighty God, and request Him to work on me as I sit still. Perfect me as a saint. Instill in me Your attributes. Enlarge my capacity for faith. Make me a productive fruitbearer for Your Spirit. Rest Your peace in me so my eyes will always be on You. And teach me the joy of Your salvation."

Because we honor rest, people who stay with us say they've never slept as well as they do in our home. Some guests who come here on retreats to seek the Lord tell us it's so peaceful, they just can't stay awake.

When we were young, neither of us honored our parents in the way the Bible instructs. It is the fifth of the Ten Commandments, and it comes with a promise: **"Honor your father and your mother, that your days may be long upon the land which the Lord your God is giving you"** (Exodus 20:12 NKJV).

When the Lord explained how our parents really did love us, we repented and realized how much they imparted to us. Now we honor their memory.

We've seen miracles of provision in our house and on our property. The Lord has multiplied resources to us. He even provided brand new sheets in the color that coordinated with the decor in one of our guest rooms. The sheets miraculously appeared a day after we looked in the same place for sheets that would work in that room. Since then we've had three other sheet miracles. Barbara believes a "sheet angel" honored us.

One day we had planned to attend an all-night prayer meeting at a church where we had never attended and knew no one. But we got in a big fight and Barbara told me to go by myself. Then she forgot why she was mad and we went happily on our way. We were some of the first ones there, and the pastor barely acknowledged us as he passed by. Then someone came in who knew us from another church and highly recommended us.

The next thing we knew, the pastor's wife, who didn't know us either, announced that we would bring a message. We spoke for over an hour (remember, it was an all-night prayer meeting), and left shortly afterward. We often laugh about this. We went to honor them and became the guest speakers. Give honor to whom it is due, and honor will come to you.

"Those who honor Me I will honor" (I Samuel 2:30 NKJV).

8

Gratitude is stewarding your future.

"As it is written [in Scripture], 'Things which the eye has not seen and the ear has not heard, and which have not entered the heart of man, all that God has prepared for those who love Him [who hold Him in affectionate reverence, who obey Him, and who gratefully recognize the benefits that He has bestowed]'" (1 Corinthians 2:9 AMP).

By Randy

The Lord has taught us many things about gratitude, such as,

"Gratitude is stewarding your future."

We had to think about this for awhile before we understood what He meant. Much of our future is determined by what we do in the present. He had already told us, **"Gratitude creates an atmosphere for increase."** So this new principle of stewarding our future is how we ensure our spiritual (not just financial) prosperity. Gratitude is good stewardship.

Once while Barbara and I were on vacation, we spent a free night in a luxurious, new hotel. The next place we stayed was not nearly as nice. A disappointed Barbara started to complain. The Lord quickly corrected her,

"If you complain, I'll have to take your blessings away from you."

We quickly changed our attitude and apologized, remembering all of His blessings instead. Complaining was being ungrateful.

God wants to prosper us. Our part is to trust Him and thank Him for how much He does for us. The poorest way to steward our future is to worry. The Lord told us:

"Don't worry about the future. Worrying can't alter it. You can only put yourself out of position to be blessed when it arrives."

The world tells us tomorrow is promised to no man, as if to suggest we can do nothing to determine whether we will see it. But to His people in Babylon who were taken as captives from Israel, God said through the prophet Jeremiah:

"'For I know the thoughts that I think toward you,' says the Lord, 'thoughts of peace and not of evil, to give you a future and a hope'" (Jeremiah 29:11 NKJV).

As a grafted-in wild olive branch and part of God's people, Christians appropriate His promises for themselves. They determine their tomorrows through their relationship with God.

The Lord once told us He has a "lovely future" ahead for His people:

"No matter what it looks like, everything that shifts in this world is leaning toward the revelation of My glory. I AM drawing all of Creation to Me.

"The humble of heart will be broken by My love, while the haughty and indignant will resist it. I have the times and seasons under control, especially for those who trust Me. Don't let worry rob you of the joy you should experience as you anticipate what I will do.

"You have a lovely future ahead of you. The thief comes to steal it with fear. Don't allow him."

The Bible says in I Thessalonians 5:18 (NKJV): **"In everything give thanks; for this is the will of God in Christ Jesus for you."**

The same God who wants to give us a lovely future tells us to be thankful in (not necessarily for) everything. That is an expression of trust. We live in times when trusting God is the only source of true peace. That enables us to see past circumstances and find good where other people cannot.

Once, the Lord told us:

"You don't know what I'm going to do in the future. You sense it's something big, but you don't know.

"If your mind is stayed on yourself, the only thing you will see when the future comes is negative. I'm going to teach you how to find the good in everything that happens.

"If you learn what I'm teaching you now, even though it seems very hard, it will be far easier than trying to learn it when your world is coming apart."

Another time, He said:

"Everything Satan brings against you will make you stronger, if you trust Me and let Me provide your needs.

"All things truly do work together for the good of those who love and trust Me, and are appointed for My purpose."

9

Get what you need and trust Me for it.

"The Lord is my best friend and my shepherd. I always have more than enough" (Psalm 23:1 TPT).

By Barbara

When God told Randy and me, **"Get what you need and trust Me for it,"** we were stunned. We knew He didn't mean for us to be impulsive, frivolous or careless. But as we understood this principle of faith, it created in us a lot of freedom. It made us realize that God is not a harsh taskmaster; He is here to help us conduct the assignments He gives us.

When it came time to buy a new laptop, we agreed to trust Him for one. We had no extra money and needed a MacBook Pro for our writing ministry. Our old laptop was reconditioned when we bought it. A short circuit kept it from holding a charge and it was at the end of its useful life.

At an appliance store, Randy asked if they had any previous models with the features we needed, still new in boxes and marked down. Yes they did, and it saved us $700. We purchased it on time payments and God provided the money to pay it off in three months.

In the old days, we needed a photocopier for the Christian newspaper Randy edited. He was using up favors from all our friends who had copiers. It put stress on relationships. We really had to have our own.

We determined to take out a loan and not pay more than $1,000. That's when the Lord told us to use tithe money. We argued with Him, "That can't be right. The Bible says the tithe needs to go into the storehouse."

He replied, **"Aren't you going to use this for the Kingdom? To spread the Gospel? Then it is going to My storehouse."**

He said anyplace that gives out the Gospel is a storehouse. That goes beyond the Church. We always thought the storehouse could only be churches. But He added, **"If a church puts money in the bank and does not use it to bring in the lost, then it's not a storehouse, it's a hoardhouse."**

A friend who has always helped with the cooking for our meetings and outreaches said, "Barbara, you need a new stove." We bought the stove we were using secondhand. It had been stored in a chickenhouse and rats had removed some the insulation.

I heard "You need a new stove" as a word from the Lord. I began to say,

9

"Lord, I need a new stove." Once a week, when I volunteered at a ministry in a nearby town, I would stop at the building supply store to check and see if the Lord had a stove for me there.

En route one day, I heard the Lord say very cheerfully, "Your stove is here today." In the meantime, I decided we also needed a refrigerator to replace our 20-year-old one. Randy protested, saying we couldn't afford it.

When I got to the store, I made a beeline to the section with the dented and dinged appliances, and there was my stove, marked way down. It just had two little blemishes. I asked if there was a marked down a refrigerator. And yes, there it was, but it had no price on it. I offered a ridiculous price, and it was accepted. Then I had to call Randy because we don't do anything without first agreeing. He protested, as usual, then said we couldn't pay more than $500 for the pair, and they could not be from a certain manufacturer.

I retorted that they were both the same brand, which Randy recognized was one of the best. And the combined cost was $500, more than half off their original price. That day they had free delivery and were giving away an icemaker along with the refrigerator. Plus, the store was reimbursing sales tax as a special incentive. The final cost was not a penny over $500.

We hold home meetings on the second floor of our house. One day our friend said she wanted to bring some "old people" (we were all in our 70s at the time), but she didn't think they could climb our steps. Then this same friend fell and broke her leg, and *she* couldn't get up our stairs either.

I heard the voice of the Lord say, "You need a stair lift." I announced to Randy, "We're getting a stair lift." He also recognized the voice of the Lord in this and agreed. That day we ordered it. We put it on a credit card.

Without asking anyone for money, the $2,400 we needed to pay for it came in before the bill arrived two weeks later. A friend installed it for free. Then I started having a lot of health and back issues and needed it for myself in addition to our company. God had provided for our own need before we even knew we needed it.

The Lord has taught us how to get what we need and trust Him for it.

"Before they call I will answer; while they are still speaking I will hear" (Isaiah 65:24 NIV).

10

Prosperity is more a matter of positioning than petitioning.

"If anyone is a worshiper of God and does His will, He hears him" (John 9:31 NKJV).

By Randy

While Barbara and I were talking in the car, the question came up, "Lord, there are people who earn two and three times as much income as we do, yet they have trouble paying their bills and their lives are unstable. Why are we doing so much better while making so much less?" His answer took us by surprise: **"Prosperity is more a matter of positioning than petitioning."**

He explained "positioning" as He gave us these **"principles as matters of stewardship"—**

"Gratitude: properly stewarding what you already have.

"Positioning: another word for obedience, which is properly stewarding what you need.

"Poverty: both financial and spiritual in nature. It is the absence of a viable relationship with Me. Notice there is a qualifier. 'Viable' means 'containing life.' A spirit of poverty can rob a man of the eternal life I want to give him, as well as abundant life – the quality of his existence on Earth.

"You can have wealth with a poverty spirit, and you can be poor and not have a poverty spirit.

"People with a spirit of poverty are not just at risk for being financially poor. Their outlook on living is destitute. They have resentment and self-doubt. Blaming is a common device to diffuse their pain. Poverty is not only found in their circumstances but their mind-set.

"How does a rich man come to poverty? People who don't manage their resources well are usually ungrateful, and that's why they suffer loss. All of the pride sins – especially poor stewardship and ingratitude – invite the devourer to take what he has.

"The flip side is the old expression, 'Little is much when God is in it.' A humble man can prosper with very little because I increase him and give him favor."

"Petition" is a word the Bible uses to mean "request." Paul wrote to the Philippians, **"Don't worry about anything, but in everything, through prayer and petition with thanksgiving, present your requests to God"** (4:6 CSB).

From what the Lord told us, we understood that prosperity is about much more than money. Perhaps the Apostle John said it best in his third epistle, **"Beloved, I pray that you may prosper in all things and be in health, just as your soul prospers"** (III John 2 NKJV).

Our souls prosper when we are in right relationship with God. That is what the Lord meant by "positioning." Genuine prosperity concerns the eternal things Jesus called **"the true riches,"** not just the material things of this world. He told His disciples:

"He who is faithful in a very little thing is also faithful in much; and he who is dishonest in a very little thing is also dishonest in much. Therefore if you have not been faithful in the use of earthly wealth, who will entrust the true riches to you? And if you have not been faithful in the use of that [earthly wealth] which belongs to another [whether God or man, and of which you are a trustee], who will give you that which is your own? No servant can serve two masters; for either he will hate the one and love the other, or he will stand devotedly by the one and despise the other. You cannot serve both God and mammon [that is, your earthly possessions or anything else you trust in and rely on instead of God]" (Luke 16:10-13 AMP).

The apostles obviously had a low opinion of worldly wealth, calling it **"filthy lucre"** numerous times in Scripture while listing qualifications for bishops, deacons and elders.

If the money we use on Earth is not considered of value in God's Kingdom, what is? The Lord explained:

"What has value in the Kingdom of God? Not the legal tender of Earth. That is merely a tool. Valued in My Kingdom are faith, obedience, righteousness, and all the attributes they entail. Character, not wealth, is the means of advancement in My Kingdom.

"On Earth, how often do you see people more miserable because they lack the character to properly steward their wealth? They proceed on the false assumption that wealth is all they need to advance. But it cannot produce peace, and its security is always temporary.

"The real fruit of wealth is fear of loss. That's why it can consume those who possess it. Joy never comes from wealth, but joy multiplies in the character of Christ.

"I'm the banker. The currency of My Kingdom is the likeness of My Son."

11

You will win more people to the cause of Christ by telling them what you're for than by telling them what you're against.

""You don't know what kind of spirit is influencing you'" (Luke 9:55 EHV).

By Randy

The controversial 1988 Hollywood movie "The Last Temptation of Christ" was playing in theaters, and many dedicated Christians were upset at this portrayal of Jesus as more carnal than divine. Locally, people looked for me to take a stand in print as editor of the regional Christian newspaper. Many were concerned that this film would be screened in our area.

I ended up writing a wishy-washy editorial that should never have been printed. Then people shifted their wrath toward me with an onslaught of complaining letters to the editor. In a parody of the hymn "Stand Up, Stand Up for Jesus," one suggested that I should "Lay Down, Lay Down for Jesus."

Everyone was angry with me. Barbara was so upset that she threatened to leave. I had been trying not to offend anyone. I didn't know it, but I was operating in a man-pleasing spirit, and ended up pleasing no one.

Eventually I learned that a man-pleasing comes from feeling insecure in God's love. It is a product of three things Satan uses to quench our faith: shame, false guilt and a sense of unworthiness.

"Fear of man is a dangerous trap, but to trust in God means safety" (Proverbs 29:25 TLB).

"We aren't trying to please people, but we are trying to please God, who continues to examine our hearts" (I Thessalonians 2:4 CEB).

I got alone with the Lord and asked how I should respond in my next edition. He said, **"You will win more people to the cause of Christ by telling them what you're for than by telling them what you're against."** Then He said, **"Now commit that movie to Me,"** adding,

"I can use anything but I don't use everything; I use those things which are committed to Me because they bring Me glory."

In my next edition, I quoted that to my readers. I explained how we, as Christians, should not take offense at others who misunderstand the testimony of Jesus. We should show them compassion. **"For the message of the cross is foolishness to those who are perishing, but to us who are being**

saved it is the power of God" (I Corinthians 1:18 NKJV).

As it turned out, "The Last Temptation of Christ" was only shown in metropolitan areas and not here. Some time later I heard that a local ministry had procured a copy of the Campus Crusade for Christ "Jesus" film, and rented a local theater which agreed to screen it. On the marquee was simply the word "Jesus." Thinking it was the other movie, so many people attended that the theater asked to hold it over for a second week at their own expense.

Ministry workers waited at theater exits to give tracts to moviegoers who had come to see something blasphemous and wound up receiving the truth.

God even used "The Last Temptation of Christ."

We live seven miles from the seaside resort of Ocean City, Maryland. Some Christian young people who stayed with us described how there were "preachers" on the boardwalk, yelling that people were going to hell. They were telling passersby what they were against, not what they were for.

Our guests said it grieved their hearts to see this. They appealed to these "preachers" to demonstrate love instead of condemnation, and the "preachers" turned on them.

Luke 6:37 (PHILLIPS) says, **"'Don't judge other people and you will not be judged yourselves. Don't condemn and you will not be condemned. Make allowances for others and people will make allowances for you.'"**

This was another example of "You will win more people to the cause of Christ by telling them what you're for than by telling them what you're against."

A personal testimony is an effective way to tell people what we are for and not what we are against. It shows God's goodness. It does not celebrate past sin but glorifies the One who set us free from sin. It demonstrates the new life we have in Him and makes it clear that all who are willing can have the same experience.

Revelation 12:11 (NKJV) says the saints overcome the evil one **"by the blood of the Lamb and by the word of their testimony."** We not only overcome him as our adversary, but with our testimonies we overcome his deception when he tries to prevent others from knowing the truth and being set free.

12

How can you get what you already have?

"My God will richly fill your every need in a glorious way through Christ Jesus" (Philippians 4:19 GW).

By Barbara

A friend who came to us for advice was unhappy with her life. Feeling deprived was interfering with her spiritual side. As we prayed, the Lord said to her through Randy, "**How can you get what you already have?**"

He was telling her that He is sufficient for everything she needs, and not to worry about it. He confirms this in Scripture :

"Have faith that you will receive whatever you ask for in prayer" (Matthew 21:22 GW).

"He who did not spare His own Son, but delivered Him up for us all, how shall He not with Him also freely give us all things?" (Romans 8:32 NKJV).

"And my God shall supply all your need according to His riches in glory by Christ Jesus" (Philippians 4:19 NKJV).

We saw God's message go right over her head because she was looking for pity, but we grabbed hold of what the Lord said. After we discussed it for several days, He showed us the meaning. He provides everything necessary, so we should look at our needs as though they are already met in Christ.

Paul wrote to the Philippians, **"And now I have it all – and keep getting more!... You can be sure that God will take care of everything you need, His generosity exceeding even yours in the glory that pours from Jesus. Our God and Father abounds in glory that just pours out into eternity. Yes"** (Philippians 4:19 MSG). If we believe this promise, we already have what we need even before it comes.

We had gone to a 6 a.m. prayer meeting, and we needed to pick up a few supplies, but it was still too early for most stores to be open. Our list included a vinyl table cloth that had to be just the right color and design, and a toilet seat.

The building supply store was open and had expensive of toilet seats, but I would not pay more than a couple dollars. When it was finally late enough for a dollar store to be open, Randy began to laugh as we pulled up. He remembered we had a new toilet seat in his shed. After searching the dollar store for a one-dollar table cloth, I was reminded that I had already bought one. It was in the laundry room, still in its cellophane packing, and it was just the right quality and color.

12

The Lord used this experience to demonstrate a spiritual principle. He truly is sufficient for all our needs, no matter how big or insignificant. We finally got the picture. At least in our case, we already had the items we needed. Now we ask ourselves if we already have what we're looking for.

Sometimes we want to treat ourselves to having dinner out or buying something extra to eat at home, and the Lord reminds us that we already have food in our pantry or freezer. This has saved us lots of money.

It is not unusual for people to ask God for more faith. His Word says He has **"dealt to every man the measure of faith"** (Romans 12:3 KJV). How can you get what you already have? Instead of asking for more, we need to become mature with what we've already been given.

We ask for healing and the Word says, **"By His stripes we are healed"** (Isaiah 53:5 NKJV, emphasis added). God wants us to know we already have it, so we must steward it. **"Whatever things you ask when you pray, believe that you receive them, and you will have them"** (Mark 11:24 NKJV).

I studied the life of George Mueller, who cared for thousands of orphans in England in the 1800s. Only to the Lord did he present their needs; he never made a public appeal. We have tried to pattern our lives after this standard.

The Bible talks about when the children of Israel went out to gather the manna in the wilderness. **"He who gathered much had nothing left over, and he who gathered little had no lack"** (Exodus 16:18 NKJV). They were to collect only enough for one day, no more. If they brought in extra, it would rot. We try to live this way so what we can stash away does not become our source – only God, who is able to provide all our needs, every single day. It requires faith.

Even though these are standards we strive for, sometimes we still get scared, even a little jealous, when other people's lives appear to go smoother or be easier than ours. Then we remind ourselves what we really believe: **"And my God shall supply all your need according to His riches in glory by Christ Jesus."** He told us:

"You can believe (in God) and still not pursue (Him). God likes to be pursued. That's why David found such favor with God, because he was a man after God's own heart."

13

Magical thinking is presumption, not faith.

"Do not be deceived, God is not mocked; for whatever a man sows, that he will also reap" (Galatians 6:7 NKJV).

By Randy

When our home equity line of credit matured and our payments tripled because we had to start paying principal on the loan, I thought to myself, "We are good people and we serve the Lord. He will do something like cause the bank to lose our paperwork, or have someone anonymously pay it off." It was a presumptuous, self-righteous interpretation of "Forgive us our debts." It was magical thinking.

Instead, for several years now, the Lord has provided resourcess to make the higher payments every month. We could never have done that without His provision. In the process, He has taught me to trust Him for our daily needs rather than expect them to be met by waving a magic wand. When He does choose to intervene in a miraculous way, it is for His glory and not a response to the delusion of "God owes me."

Now I ask myself, "What made me think we could borrow money without paying it back?" Ecclesiastes 5:5 (MSG) says, **"Far better not to vow in the first place than to vow and not pay up."** And Psalm 37:21 (NKJV) says, **"The wicked borrows and does not repay."**

This is true not only of money. Sometimes when people want the same anointing as someone else, they don't want to endure the inconvenience, sacrifice or waiting it takes. They believe they can receive it just for the asking, without any effort on their part. That is magical thinking.

On the Internet, Barbara found this explanation of magical thinking:

"You can't pray for an 'A' on a test and study for a 'C.' You can't pray for a faithful relationship and live an unfaithful life. The moral of the story: You can't pray for something and act less. Don't question God and His abilities when your actions don't match you prayers."

Magical thinking is entitlement and a religious spirit. A woman from Texas called us because no one was attending her Bible studies. We asked if she advertised them or put up posters. No. She was disappointed because she expected the Holy Spirit to direct people to attend, so she did not need to announce it. It was magical thinking.

Another person we know was very outspoken about her faith in the workplace, even to the point of being disruptive. She worked for an influential government agency and made a good salary, yet she did not pay her bills. She lost her car, the place where she and her children were living, and eventually her job. Her attitude was, "I am a mature Christian and I should not be denied, rejected, or suffer loss." She considered herself to be persecuted for righteousness' sake. It was entitlement – magical thinking.

God said to us, "Magical thinking is presumption, not faith. Presumption is when you assume something is true and act on it. Many times, presumption produces a sense of entitlement, which is when people claim what they suppose are their rights.

"You can see room in this thinking for delusion and abuse. When done in the name of faith, it assumes justification. When done in the name of religion, this thinking believes no one can contradict it. A person with magical thinking may believe his faith is in God when it is really asserting what he believes he deserves."

People try to fit God in their boxes, and even quote Scripture to remind Him of His promises, as if He owes them. God will provide our needs, but not without first establishing truth and accountability.

When He said to us, "There are no formulas and no guarantees," He was not contradicting Scripture. His meaning was that we cannot interpret His Word selectively as a way to get what we desire. God does not want us to believe we can manipulate Him, because we'd be tempted to treat Him as a vending machine instead of our Creator and Heavenly Father who loves us.

When the Lord first told us about magical thinking, we recognized that it could be another form of "name it and claim it." Rather than standing on the assurances in God's Word, our thinking can easily fall into presumption, which bankrupts our faith.

Too often, we think that our necessities can be provided through an infusion of money., so that's what we pray for. God can use many things to supply our wants and needs besides what He calls "filthy lucre."

He once told us, "It insults Me when people only ask for money when they have so many other needs. They are treating Me as if I were the god Mammon."

14

Don't rebel against common sense.

"A godly man gives good advice, but a rebel is destroyed by lack of common sense" (Proverbs 10:21 TLB).

By Randy

As I was preparing for bed after a long, exhausting day, I said to myself, "I'm too tired to even brush my teeth." Then I heard the Lord say, **"Don't rebel against common sense."**

The next day, Barbara and I discussed this and began to think about other ways we might rebel against common sense.

Common sense is an attribute of wisdom. Proverbs 3:13-15 (TLB) says, **"The man who knows right from wrong and has good judgment and common sense is happier than the man who is immensely rich! For such wisdom is far more valuable than precious jewels. Nothing else compares with it."**

The book of Proverbs is sometimes called the "wisdom book." In Proverbs 8:35-36, the voice of Wisdom says, **"For whoever finds me finds life, and obtains favor from the Lord; but he who sins against me wrongs his own soul; all those who hate me love death"** (NKJV).

If a small matter such as not brushing teeth is rebelling against common sense, what about bigger things? Whenever we disobey God in anything, we rebel against common sense. To recognize that fact, it is necessary to believe that God has our best interest at heart, and that His commandments and ordinances are intended to protect us, not to shackle us.

It is not uncommon for lost people to view God's laws as something He demands for the sake of His reputation, not for our well-being. That is a result of not trusting Him. The wisdom of common sense assures us that His desire is to protect us from the consequences of violating these principles. Even when we are forgiven, there are still consequences for rebelling against common sense.

"Do not be deceived, God is not mocked; for whatever a man sows, that he will also reap" (Galatians 6:7 NKJV).

A practical example of rebelling against common sense is when people have lost their houses but could easily have kept them. Our daughter, who is a realtor, has told us stories about people who believed God would make their house payments for them, so they made no effort themselves. They thought it was faith, but it was really presumption and a form of entitlement, which was rebelling against common sense.

14

In some of these cases, the creditor had made provision for them to keep their houses by offering to restructure their mortgages so they could afford them. There are laws to help these people, but they remained in denial, continuing to rebel against common sense.

Many became mad at God for not pulling them out of the situation they created themselves. Some whose houses went to foreclosure vandalized them out of resentment, or left the houses filthy and uninhabitable. This, of course, goes against the "Golden Rule" we learned as children: **"Do unto others as you would have others do unto you"** (Luke 6:31 MEV).

A woman asked Barbara to pray for her because she was having erotic nightmares. Barbara asked if she was watching soap operas on TV, and her answer was yes. Then Barbara remembered they had the same conversation almost a year earlier. Barbara again told her to stop, because soap operas were the open door which let in her nightmares. The woman didn't have common sense to listen and be obedient the first time, even after she asked for help. Hopefully she did the second time.

The more I thought about the idea of rebelling, the more it scared me. I remembered I Samuel 15:23, **"For rebellion is as the sin of witchcraft, and stubbornness is as iniquity and idolatry"** (NKJV).

Who would want to be guilty of witchcraft in God's eyes? And if failing to observe common sense is a form of stubbornness, who would want to be guiltly of idolatry? Idolatry is when we give God's rightful place in our hearts to anything or anyone else besides Him.

The Bible calls this harlotry, and it is one of the major offenses God warns us about in His commandments. It is putting another god before Him. It is the god of Self – our own will.

What the Lord told me is a call not just for me but for everyone to examine himself and ask—

How am I rebelling against common sense?

15

Back out of the corner and keep your eyes on what is accomplished, not what remains.

"Let your eyes look straight ahead, and your eyelids look right before you. Ponder the path of your feet, and let all your ways be established. Do not turn to the right or the left"

(Proverbs 4:25-27 NKJV).

By Barbara

When we designed our house, we included a first floor apartment for my daughter. Eventually, she and her husband built their own house and moved out, and the apartment became a sewing studio for my banner ministry and a storage area.

I had long tables with piles and piles of sorted fabrics and accessories. It was also a repository for many other things.

One day someone asked to rent the apartment, and we needed the extra income. But as I looked at all the stuff that had to be removed to make it livable, I was totally overwhelmed. It was a daunting task.

In a state of depression and self-pity, I asked the Lord to help me. That's when He said, **"Back out of the corner and keep your eyes on what is accomplished, not what remains to be done."**

He instructed me to go to the far corner, take things out and put them in other places, keeping likes with likes. Using this method, I was able to complete the cleanup without being intimidated. This way, I was always looking at a part that was finished and I felt like I was accomplishing something, even though it took many days.

This goes along with when He told us:

"Do the next thing."

Instead of looking ahead to all that needed to be accomplished, I learned to just take them one at a time, and it gave me peace.

We have come to understand the importance of doing things in their proper sequence. The Lord told us to pray that we **"get more done in less time with less effort."**

Even though this has been said by many others, it impacted us when God said it. We often repeat it to each other when we are working on big projects. It prevents us from going on rabbit trails, keeps us focused, and helps us not be overpowered by the size of the job.

Whether we're writing something or building something or whatever we're doing, we focus on these principles so we can be more effective with our efforts and efficient with our time.

The Lord has instructed me many times not to place too much emphasis on the dictates of the clock and the calendar. He has told me to see **"with eyes of eternity."** This puts the demands of the world in perspective. It helps me determine what is truly important, and keeps me from worry.

Yet time is a non-renewable resource. The psalmist asked God to **"teach us to numbers our days"** (Psalm 90:12 KJV), and we must make wise use of the time we have on Earth.

We need to be reminded of the words in James 4:14, **"For your fleeting life is but a warm breath of air that is visible in the cold only for a moment and then vanishes!"** (TPT).

I think of all that the Apostle Paul endured. Still, he pressed **"toward the goal for the prize of the upward call of God in Christ Jesus"** (Philippians 3:14 NKJV) until he could confidently say, **"I have finished the race. I have kept the faith"** (II Timothy 4:7 NKJV).

To accomplish this, sometimes we have to back out of the corner.

If the amount of work we have to do doesn't overwhelm us, there are occasions when the condition of the world does. When we look around us, sometimes we can't draw confidence from what we have accomplished by backing out of the corner. We have to fix our gaze on Jesus, the Author and Finisher of our faith (Hebrews 12:2).

His words to the disciples just before He went to the cross ring true for us as well: **"In the world you will have tribulation; but be of good cheer, I have overcome the world"** (John 16:33 NKJV)

The lyrics of the Alan Jackson hymn remind us:

Turn your eyes upon Jesus,
Look full in His wonderful face,
And the things of Earth will grow strangely dim,
In the light of His glory and grace.

16

"Rise up with wings like eagles" means learning to soar instead of flap.

"But they who wait upon the Lord will get new strength. They will rise up with wings like eagles. They will run and not get tired. They will walk and not become weak"

(Isaiah 40:31 NLV).

By Randy

There is comfort in the passage that says, "**Those who wait on the Lord shall renew their strength; they shall mount up with wings like eagles, they shall run and not be weary, they shall walk and not faint**" (Isaiah 40:31 NKJV).

This verse has always painted an encouraging picture, but I wonder what it would look like for me to "mount up with wings like eagles." The Lord explained it when He said, "**'Rise up with wings like eagles' means learning to soar instead of flap.**"

In college, I took a broadcasting course that was taught by an affable, old-timey radio announcer who guaranteed us a grade of "C" just for coming to class. And every assignment I turned in also got a "C." I was discouraged because I worked long hours to produce complex projects and achieve professional quality, only to be told what I did was average.

So I concluded, "What's the sense of knocking myself out if I'll get the same grade either way?" The next tape I submitted was called "The History of Sound Effects in Radio." I scrounged an old sound effects record (this was way before CDs) and mixed it with a hastily written script. The whole undertaking took less than an hour to prepare.

To my amazement, I was given a "B+" on something that I thought was slapped together. I learned a lesson which preceded me in life for 50 years. I have to guard against making things harder than they need to be.

I think that is what the Lord meant by "**learning to soar instead of flap.**" The perfectionist in me may not visibly procrastinate, but it will keep pursuing something until it seems perfect, often working past the point of diminishing returns by investing too much time and effort. That is when I need to soar instead of flap.

When writing features for the Christian newspaper I edited, I certainly wanted to give the Lord my best. I would record interviews, transcribe them, and write articles from my notes. Then I went over them again and again to get the wording just right. I was correcting things no one else would notice. My dad used to call that "running it into the ground."

16

I was spending lots of energy on things that ultimately didn't matter, flapping as hard as I could. I had to learn to relax and not focus on what made little or no difference. I had to learn to soar.

The Bible calls soaring "resting in the Lord." It means *to look for, trust, and hope in Him.* Psalm 37 illustrates it best:

"Trust in the Lord, and do good; dwell in the land, and feed on His faithfulness. Delight yourself also in the Lord, and He shall give you the desires of your heart. Commit your way to the Lord, trust also in Him, and He shall bring it to pass. He shall bring forth your righteousness as the light, and your justice as the noonday. Rest in the Lord, and wait patiently for Him…." (vss. 3-7 NKJV)

Resting in the Lord – soaring – is a conscious, deliberate decision. It's not the result of being passive or indifferent. The Lord has told Barbara and me we must learn to rest in Him. He said:

"Every moment contains choices. Whenever you make a choice, you exercise a right. A slave has no choice but to do what he's told because he has no rights. Exercising the right to make choices is a hallmark of being a son.

"Resting in Me is a choice. You decide to trust Me with everything and not worry about anything. You tell Me your needs and you are grateful for My generosity. When you determine to trust Me in everything, you give Me your whole heart. Logic no longer directs you toward fear. Instead, My peace guards your heart as it reassures your mind.

"It doesn't even have to make sense for you to have peace. It is a joy that rises above circumstances because it captures your whole being, not just your mind.

"The best example of such joy was the eagerness of Jesus to complete His mission, even knowing what it would require. Although His suffering was greater than any man's, He spurned fear by looking ahead to the salvation it would purchase.

"Rest is joy because when you are at rest, you can think about Me. When you're busy, you have hundreds of distractions competing for your attention. It's good to rest now and again."

17

The more you say it, the more it happens.

"Death and life are in the power of the tongue, and those who love it will eat its fruit" (Proverbs 18:21 NKJV).

By Randy

"God, You're so good." It surprised Barbara and me when the Lord directed us to repeat that statement often. Saying it came naturally, so why was it necessary for Him to instruct us? **"The more you say it, the more it happens,"** He said.

It wasn't a lack of reverence in our attitudes. Of course He is worthy of our praise. God was positioning us for blessings. He was showing us about the power of our words.

By speaking blessings, we receive blessings. Proverbs 18:20 says, **"People will be rewarded for what they say; they will be rewarded by how they speak"** (NCV).

God has made man unique among all life on Earth. We have the authority to co-create with Him, and He has given us speech to accomplish it. The next verse in Proverbs says, **"Death and life are in the power of the tongue, and those who love it will eat its fruit"** (18:21 NKJV).

That is why Jesus said we will give an account on the Day of Judgment for every idle word we speak (Matthew 12:36). Our words are so powerful that we must steward them wisely and not waste them.

The Lord has given Barbara and me prayers to say. At first we thought it unusual. If He already knows what we should pray, why do we need to say it? He wanted us to use the authority of our words. It says in Job, **"You will also decide and decree a thing, and it will be established for you..."** (22:28 AMP).

These are the declarations He told us to make every day:

- **I see today as an opportunity.**
- **I will stand fast.**
- **My faith shall not be moved.**
- **I declare my strength is in the Lord, and that He is faithful.**
- **I declare my joy does not depend on other people, but it comes from the Lord.**
- **Even my sorrows are but light afflictions which make the way for God's glory to be revealed in me.**

17

• I see God's hand at work so my circumstances don't become my whole world.

• I know with assurance that God us in all of the situations I can think of, to produce a good outcome for everyone involved.

• I perceive that reality is not what my senses detect; reality is the unshakable truth of God's Word.

• I declare that as my faith is tested, I will grow into the measure of God's joy for me.

The Lord was teaching us to bless ourselves with the authority of our own mouth. And the more we say it, the more it happens. He added these:

• God has chosen me out of the world and I belong to Him.

• I am greatly blessed, highly favored and deeply loved.

• I have God's sufficiency, power and authority.

• He gives me wisdom, influence and favor.

• I choose peace today. I am a peacemaker.

• I will not give power to evil by submitting to fear.

• Joy is my compass for today and I am grateful.

• I live in the Kingdom of God, which is righteousness, peace and joy in the Holy Spirit.

• I declare I am a son in God's Kingdom. I trust God to provide my needs because He has my best interest at heart. I accept where He has me and trust where He is taking me. I want to please Him with faith and position myself for what He wants to do. I need His help to do this.

• I pray my day be even, not letting extremes weary or stress me but letting peace guide me today. I am not under control of my circumstances but take authority over the most challenging situations. Help me let joy infiltrate my heart, peace dictate my thoughts, and love craft my words.

* I commend my family members to God's grace and authority and request Him to perfect us as saints, instill in us His attributes, enlarge our capacities for faith, make us productive fruitbearers for His Spirit, rest His peace in us so our eyes will always be on Him, and teach us the joy of His salvation.

18

Wisdom, influence and favor can get more done than hard work, if you trust Me.

"Trust in and rely confidently on the Lord with all your heart and do not rely on your own insight or understanding. In all your ways know and acknowledge and recognize Him, and He will make your paths straight and smooth [removing obstacles that block your way]" (Proverbs 3:5-6 AMP).

By Barbara

We have always been hard workers. Of the two of us, Randy admits to being less motivated to work. That is one difference between men and women, he says, because he has never met a "lazy" woman.

I kept hearing from the Lord that I should rest, but I didn't know how. So when ailments kept me from doing physical labor, Randy had to do his work plus mine.

The Lord told us, **"Wisdom, influence and favor can get more done than hard work, *if you trust Me.*"** I have prayed that almost daily. When the Lord gives you something to pray, He will prove Himself faithful.

Randy did all the work for both of us, and to our surprise, more was actually getting done than before.

Wisdom is the *feat* of the Lord. *Feat* is defined as "an achievement that requires great courage, skill, or strength." Influence is the outcome of giving and servanthood. And favor results from having a good track record.

"Let not mercy and truth forsake you; bind them around your neck, write them on the tablet of your heart, and so find favor and high esteem in the sight of God and man" (Proverbs 3:3-4 NKJV).

As part of my income when I was a single mom, I had painted many murals for establishments in nearby Ocean City. I also did complimentary signs, murals and decorating for almost every ministry in our area. I did it as unto the Lord. This gave me favor with God. And with my own income, I bought carpet, vinyl flooring, appliances, furniture and personal items for those in need. I drew up blueprints for buildings and gave thousands of dollars to help other ministries. This gave me favor with many people.

"A man's gift makes room for him, and brings him before great men" (Proverbs 18:16 NKJV).

God has had us connect many people to each other. Then they go out and do the work we normally would have done, but are now unable to do. He has sent the very best to take up where we left off. We've watched Him encourage and direct people through our words, and we are actually seeing **more get done with less effort in less time** (another prayer God gave us).

There is a season when you have to do all the labor yourself. Then there comes a time when you let go of the work and the Lord has you mentor others who will start where you stopped. This has been a rewarding season, watching others go far beyond where the Lord took us.

When Randy pioneered the Christian newspaper he edited for 25 years, he began as a staff of one. He wrote, edited, proofread, produced and delivered it, often working more than 60 hours a week. Eventually the radio station which published it hired people to help him so he could focus on the areas in which he was best qualified. People came alongside him to make the paper more efficient because Randy had wisdom, influence and favor.

The Lord also told us, "You have My sufficiency, power and authority." That holds true for all His children. When we led prayer incursions in our region, we embraced that statement so we were not held back by fear of inadequacy. And God responded. So when we pray now, it's not about us. We look to be in agreement with God's purposes, declare them on the earth, and wait to see the results.

This principle was demonstrated when friends of ours needed to have their expensive German car repaired. The estimate was $5,000, so they agreed to give the car to the mechanic rather than pay that much, since it was a third vehicle.

A little later, the wife heard the Lord say, "Go get your car." So she went back to the garage and asked about it. They had only done $600 of the needed work, so she paid the bill and got the car back, even though she and her husband had both signed over the title. That was God's favor. Then she sold the car for $3,000, making a profit of $2,400 rather than losing the car altogether.

The wisdom and favor of God turned their potential loss into gain.

In Proverbs 8:17 (NKJV), Wisdom says, **"I love those who love me, and those who seek me diligently will find me."**

According to Psalm 1:1-3 (NKJV), **"Blessed is the man who walks not in the counsel of the ungodly, nor stands in the path of sinners, nor sits in the seat of the scornful; but his delight is in the law of the Lord, and in His law he meditates day and night. He shall be like a tree planted by the rivers of water, that brings forth its fruit in its season, whose leaf also shall not wither; and whatever he does shall prosper."**

That is the keynote scripture for Shiloh Ministries.

19

Don't think good or bad, right or wrong; think wise or foolish, obedient or disobedient.

"Judge not, and you shall not be judged. Condemn not, and you shall not be condemned" (Luke 6:37 NKJV).

By Randy

A long time ago, Barbara frequently underwent self-condemnation by thinking she was doing something bad or wrong. She would tell herself, "I'm stupid." One day, the Lord told us not to think in terms of good or bad, right or wrong; but to view things as wise or foolish, obedient or disobedient.

Good/bad, right/wrong implies judgment and disapproval. Wise/foolish, obedient/disobedient is an observation without condemnation.

When we built our house, the property the Lord provided was adjacent to a denominational church believed by many to be a cult. That fear came on us too, so after buying the lot we poured a gallon of olive oil around its border and declared it as the blood of Jesus to defend against what we imagined would be the spiritual pollution of false doctrine. After we marched around the perimeter, prayed, and declared everything we could think of to safeguard our land, we asked the Lord how we should respond to the people from this church.

"I don't require you to be right," He said, "I require you to show mercy. Whenever you think you're right, it means someone else has to be wrong, and that is pride. I resist the proud but give grace to the humble."

Since then we have met people who attend churches which many Christians believe are in error. Rather than debate theology with them, the Lord has instructed us to pray "that the love of God indwell their meetings and the people who attend them, and the love of God come in the power of His Spirit to lead them into all truth."

No judgment or self-promotion or pride on our part, just blessings over them.

Out of my love for Barbara, I called her from a computer show to tell her about a screen printing machine she could use in her banner making ministry. It was $4,000, a sum we really could not afford, but we both agreed on it.

We later realized it was a poor investment because we lacked the skill to properly use it, and we gave it to our son who used it a few times. Then he gave it to a friend who was able to use it some. We never saw it again.

19

It was a foolish purchase, but the Lord told us not to condemn ourselves by saying it was bad or wrong. Because we agreed, we were obedient to the principle of not doing anything without being in one accord. That way we wouldn't blame each other, and it would become a lesson learned rather than a source of contention.

We had the same kind of experience several more times. With our daughter, we bought a house to fix and flip, and made $20,000. Then we bought another house to fix and flip, the market tanked, and we lost $20,000.

We were in agreement going in, so it didn't cause a rift between us, but we gained wisdom that this was not something we were gifted for and we should not do it again.

Later we lost $8,000 in three months in a ministry endeavor, but because we purposed not to do anything unless we were in agreement, it did not cause division.

We make unwise judgments when we say "good/bad, right/wrong." Often, when we think we are judging someone else's actions or our own, we are judging the person himself instead.

Romans 14:4 (GW) says, **"Who are you to criticize someone else's servant? The Lord will determine whether his servant has been successful."**

Because some of our mistakes were costly and foolish, we learned to love wisdom and obedience. We check in with the Lord to make sure we are where we're supposed to be and doing what we're supposed to do. He has taught us to pray from a place of humility, not fear.

And He has repeatedly said to us, **"Trust Me to tell you if you are veering to the right or the left. If I don't tell you, that means you are exactly where I want you to be."**

20

Where do you hurt, and where do you hide?

"'I heard Your voice in the garden, and I was afraid because I was naked; and I hid myself'" (Genesis 3:10 NKJV).

By Randy

A young couple called to ask for counseling. They were unstable in their marriage and their ministry. They relocated often. In my heart I was judgmental, but I did not want to bruise them with critical advice. So I asked the Lord what to say. He responded, **"Don't ask them what they have done and what they haven't done. Ask, 'Where do you hurt, and where do you hide?'"**

While I made a mental note of what to say to them, I also looked inside myself to see if the same question applied to me. I was reminded of once when I was in church. At the time, I was editor of a Christian newspaper which covered a three-state area. People recognized my name. I was smug. As I sat in my self-righteousness, I heard a quiet voice say inside me, **"You're hiding in here."** I knew exactly what it meant – I was not pursuing a deeper relationship with God. I was sitting in His house, hiding from *Him*!

Recalling that incident launched me on a search. Why do we hide?

The first instance of hiding was Adam and Eve in the Garden of Eden. They had eaten the forbidden fruit, realized they were naked, and hid from God. It wasn't only an awareness that they were without clothing, which they had never seen. They perceived that the mantle of God's glory which had covered them was gone. Now their flesh had to provide its own protection. They recognized nakedness as vulnerability, became afraid, and hid. Man has been trying to hide from God ever since. All hiding is ultimately from God.

Why do we think we can hide from Him? In Jeremiah 23:24, the Lord asks, **"'Can anyone hide himself in secret places, so I shall not see him?' says the Lord; 'do I not fill heaven and earth?' says the Lord"** (NKJV).

We hide because we fear and we hide because we hurt. The first man and woman hurt because they had exchanged life for death, and they surrendered the authority God gave them to Satan, whose name mean "adversary."

Hiding is demonic. Demons try to hide where and what they are. Men try to hide from God in the world that accommodates their fears. It's the only place dark enough that they think He won't see them there. John wrote that men **"loved darkness instead of light because their deeds were evil. Everyone who does evil hates the light, and will not come into the light for fear that their deeds will be exposed"** (John 3:19-20 NIV).

Men act as the world acts to conceal themselves. And the world accepts its own by telling them it's okay to ignore God. Repentance is the only thing that changes the way we act. It is not just telling God we're sorry and asking His forgiveness – it is a shift in how we think, which transforms how we behave.

Before I repented and was spiritually reborn, I hid in the world. I identified with bad people. To fit in, I tried to be like them, secretly believing I was superior so I could feel good about myself. I hid because, deep inside, I feared failure and I feared success. Failure generated rejection, and success might require more than I wanted to give.

Now I see hiding for what it is – SELFISHNESS. And I recognize the things I have hidden behind and why. When I feel insecure, I'm still tempted to use them as a smokescreen. Can you relate to any of these?

• **Intellectualism/religion** – talking about heady ideas to make an impression without making a commitment.

• **Abilities/giftedness** – finding identity in what I do rather than who God says I am.

• **Self-pity** – entitlement pandering for sympathy.

• **Unforgiveness** – inability to release the past.

• **Shame** – feeds fear and an orphan mind-set.

• **Perfectionism/procrastination** – waiting until conditions are perfect before moving ahead.

• **Man-pleasing** – changing who I am to meet the expectations of others and manipulate them.

• **Church** – putting in an appearance to be seen by men.

• **Ministry** – using position as a front to impress rather than a platform to serve.

• **Duty** – Joyless obedience which reduces Christianity to just another belief system.

• **Personal appearance** – relying on how I look (good or bad) so people won't see the real me.

• **Entertainment** – making life about gratifying myself rather than pleasing God.

• **Resisting/stubbornness** – the opposite of being humble and teachable.

21

Think big and look long.

"Where there is no vision,
the people perish"
(Proverbs 29:18 KJV).

By Barbara

I have been blessed with an active imagination and great vision. When I gave my life totally to the Lord, I said, "I'm going to read the Bible, believe it and do it." I had a source for vision right there in the pages of Scripture.

One of the first things I read was that our children shall inherit the land. I Chronicles 28:8 says, **"Be careful to seek out all the commandments of the Lord your God, that you may possess this good land, and leave it as an inheritance for your children after you forever"** (NKJV).

I interpreted it to mean that if they would inherit the land, I would too. As a single mother of three children who only earned $3,000 the previous year, I believed God would provide for me to buy my very own house.

That's exactly what happened. I believed it and He did it. I was thinking big and looking long. Thinking big was that I could buy a house. Looking long was buying a house as an investment, instead of renting a house and never getting a return on the payments.

I was 34 when I bought a five-bedroom, 100-year-old house. When Randy was 29, before we were married, he too bought a house rather than pay rent. When we sold his house years later, we made a nice profit.

The Bible says, **"Where there is no vision, the people perish"** (Proverbs 29:19 KJV). Vision is thinking big and looking long. If we lack vision, we get stuck and waste away like unpicked fruit.

My experience has also inspired others to buy or build houses. One of our friends lived with her two adolescent sons in a rundown shack with a hole in the kitchen floor and no working plumbing. They had to bathe in a nearby pond. It was pretty miserable. But through encouragement and her own ingenuity and lots of hard work, she and her sons built their own house.

In my first house, as a single mom, I took in more than two dozen people in four years who needed a place to live. Now, Randy and I live in the house God told us to build, and we continue to think big and look long. We have had hundreds of overnight guests. Because we cooked food at home for free meals in Ocean City, we have fed thousands out of our kitchen.

We are always looking for ways to sleep one more person, to fit one more guest at our table, to create one more parking place, to squeeze in one more chair for our house meetings – all this on one-third of an acre. This is part of the way we think big and look long to advance God's Kingdom.

Advancing the Kingdom on Earth is a the theme throughout the Bible, from the dominion mandate in Genesis 1 to the last chapter of Revelation.

"Then God blessed them, and God said to them, 'Be fruitful and multiply; fill the earth and subdue it; have dominion over the fish of the sea, over the birds of the air, and over every living thing that moves on the earth'" (Genesis 1:28 NKJV).

"'And behold, I am coming quickly, and My reward is with Me, to give to every one according to his work. I am the Alpha and the Omega, the Beginning and the End, the First and the Last'" (Revelation 22:12-13 NKJV).

This instruction from the Lord applies not only to us but to everyone:

"I tell you to think big and look long, not to satisfy your personal needs but to recognize how everything you do speaks of eternity to those around you.

"I say think big because your big thinking is too small. I say look long because immediate needs are clouding your distant vision. Let Me stretch you, prepare you and teach you. I want to put you on display.

"When you consider how few people know to do this, you can see how privileged you are to be counted among My sons (male and female). You are My emissaries to this world.

"In your new season, more and more people are watching you. They will find what they need in Me as they look at you. I want to use you as My example. I want to reveal My love to others by lavishing it on you. I want you to be special. I want you to feel special. I want you to receive people's attempts to treat you as special.

"You'll have to get over some of the things you are self-conscious about and things which frighten you – things in yourself and uncertainty about the future. If you whine or bellyache, you will watch your witness scatter like powder. Thankfulness, joy and peace will earn you more authority than being correct.

"Looking with eyes full of eternity will make you more effective in the things of the present. I have a wonderful future planned for you. You will like it if you do this My way."

22

Faith is a noun. Trust is a verb.

"Trust in the Lord with all your heart,
and lean not on your own understanding;
in all your ways acknowledge Him,
and He shall direct your paths"
(Proverbs 3:5-6 NKJV).

By Randy

Since the day I responded to an altar call and asked Jesus to be the Lord and Savior of my life, God has been teaching me about trusting Him. He taught me, **"Faith is a noun, trust is a verb."** Trust is an action.

Romans 12:3 (NKJV) says, **"God has dealt to each one a measure of faith."** So it's not whether we *have* faith but whether we *use* the faith we have. That is the deliberate act of trusting God, and it's our choice. Our lives on Earth are lived in a laboratory where tests are conducted to see if we will walk by that faith or rely on our own understanding.

I was a typical boy who took things apart to see what made them work. That's how I learned to fix things. It's part of male nature. But relying on my own ability to understand has gotten me into trouble, too. Twice, the book of Proverbs cautions against relying on our own ability to understand: **"There is a way that seems right to a man, but its end is the way of death"** (14:12, 16:25 NKJV).

Faith is when we trust God in the things we don't understand. We know He answers prayer, but sometimes we don't understand *the way* He does it.

As a single parent, Barbara was able to buy a five-bedroom house right in town. Even though it was almost 100 years old, it was in good shape. The only big problem was the heat. For a furnace, it used an old-fashioned boiler which barely produced heat throughout the house. She and her children had to sit huddled around a rickety firebox in one of the living rooms. Because it was rusted through in places, it was very dangerous. They prayed for God's help because they had no money to make improvements.

One cold winter night, a fire started in the furnace room. The firehouse was only a block away and firefighters responded quickly, containing the damage to that one area. It was a blessing in disguise. Even though Barbara and the kids had to clean up the soot, insurance repaired the damage and replaced the boiler with a new furnace. They had great heat from then on. What looked like a loss turned out to be a great gain.

Our peace is the barometer of how much we trust God. Paul wrote to the Philippians, **"Be anxious for nothing, but in everything by prayer and supplication, with thanksgiving, let your requests be made known to God; and the peace of God, which surpasses all understanding, will guard your**

hearts and minds through Christ Jesus" (4:6-7 NKJV).

The opposite of trust is worry. The Lord told us about that:

"I want you to prosper. To do so, you must be able to receive the answers to prayer. Worry will hold up answers to prayer faster than anything, even the devil.

"When you expect from the future, you can receive either of two things: answered prayer or anxiety. Answers to prayer sometimes require waiting, but you can have anxiety right away.

"Learning to wait develops character and glorifies Me. Worry puts you first and develops illness.

"Because the process of waiting makes what you receive sufficient, it is always satisfying. When you are anxious, nothing satisfies because whatever arrives is never enough.

"I want to give you better and more elaborate than you can imagine or hope for. The more patient you are, the quicker it will come. Waiting on Me extends your faith from a single situation to many aspects of your life. It builds you up to trust Me in everything.

"Anxiety spreads like gangrene, and soon, all areas of your existence are consumed with worry. That's how anxiety nullifies your faith.

"Trusting Me is its own reward. Anxiety is its own punishment."

The Lord added a precaution to this message:

"There are many people who attempt to live by faith, yet they don't understand what their faith is in. These people don't have a faith walk, they have a religion walk. Living by faith is trusting Me in everything.

"Trust is not just a virtue; trust is an action. Trust makes you acknowledge in whom you trust. Most men trust themselves, some men trust other men, but I will pick and use those who trust Me.

"I have all things seen and unseen, and I AM not a selfish God. I wait with eternal patience to give My Kingdom to those who trust Me and in whom I can trust.

"All heaven and earth are yours, and as I have given to you, I will give to every man, woman and child who trusts Me."

23

You don't get healthy by reading an exercise book. You have to do the exercises.

"Study to show yourself approved by God,
a workman who need not be ashamed,
rightly dividing the word of truth"
(II Timothy 2:15 MEV).

By Randy

I was 33 when the depravity of a selfish lifestyle made me look over my shoulder at the years I had wasted. I didn't know what it meant to be "saved," but I knew I wasn't.

That thought was constantly before me, scaring me. I had heard that Jesus would return one day. I was afraid of going to hell.

Then I ran into my old friend (soon to become my best friend) Barbara. We started dating. I would take us out into the middle of the inland bay in my little whaler and kill the motor, and she would tell me about Jesus.

A teacher was leading Bible studies in her house, and I began attending. When I tried to read the Scriptures at home, I could understand the words but I didn't comprehend their significance. The teacher told me to pray before reading and ask the Holy Spirit to reveal the meaning. That was easy enough.

I had purchased a Lamsa Bible, translated directly from the ancient manuscripts and purported to be very accurate. I was about to read the account of the Crucifixion in John 19. First I prayed that I would understand the message.

When I was growing up, my whole family went to church. I heard the stories from the Bible, including the life of Jesus. This time, as I read the old, old story, I experienced an emotional response to it. I had never before cried over a book. But as John described the toment and agony of the cross, I became aware of Jesus' love for me as an individual, not just as a face in the crowd or an element of His Creation. I realized for the first time that He would have given His life for me alone.

Even though I said a sinner's prayer at an altar call weeks later, I think I was really saved during that experience of reading the Word for the first time with understanding. After that, I spent hours each day in my Bible. It was the first time in my life I was spiritually hungry.

Barbara and I had been married for several years when she came into my home office one day and said matter-of-factly, "You're not interceding in the Spirit for me and the children." It wasn't an accusation, just a statement. I couldn't dispute it. This prompted me to study the Bible and see what it means to be the priest of my family and the head of my household.

23

As I looked in the Scriptures, I Timothy 3:5 (NKJV) got my attention—

"For if a man does not know how to rule his own house, how will he take care of the church of God?"

I studied that verse word by word. Among the meanings attributed to "rule" is "to put ahead of other things." It doesn't mean to run with an iron fist or to always have the last word, as I had thought. It means to serve sacrificially. The household head is to bring his family into the Kingdom of God, and bring God's Kingdom into his family.

After seeming to stall following my salvation experience, my spiritual growth began to accelerate. I understood that God requires a lot from the family priest, and also gives him a great allowance of grace and wisdom for the job. I was reading the exercise book and learning to do the exercises.

Once when Barbara and I got into a big fight and she was prepared to leave, I got alone with the Lord and asked Him what happened. That's when He gave me what we learned to call The Mirror Image Principle: "Your relationship with your wife is a mirror image of your relationship with Me. So if you're having problems, don't look at her. Look at yourself. Get your relationship right with Me and I'll take care of the woman."

I protested my innocence and tried to defend myself to the Lord, but He wasn't taking sides. He put the ball squarely in my court by telling me:

"From now on, you're not allowed to have another critical thought about your wife or say another unkind word to her. You keep your nose in the Word and your mind in prayer and get your relationship right with Me, and let Me take care of her."

He was saying to study the Scriptures and pursue Him. It was II Timothy 2:15, **"Work hard so you can present yourself to God and receive His approval. Be a good worker, one who does not need to be ashamed and who correctly explains the Word of Truth"** (NLT).

The truth was, I had harbored a spirit of resentment since I was a child. Resentment makes you take out your frustrations on the people closest to you, so I had to be delivered from it. We later concluded that our marriage had been born again when I was healed from resentment. Getting healthy came from doing the exercises.

24

Help me to discern Your voice, recognize Your will and do the work.

"Your ears shall hear a word behind you, saying, 'This is the way, walk in it'" (Isaiah 30:21 NKJV).

By Barbara

The Lord taught us to pray, **"Help me to discern Your voice, recognize Your will and do the work."**

The voice we hear can be our own or someone else's, even that of the enemy. But we want to hear God's voice. I find that whenever I get confused or stuck, if I just stop and be still, the Lord will show me what to do. He told Randy and me that He wants to talk to us more than we want to talk to Him.

Jesus described Himself in John 10 as the Good Shepherd whose sheep follow Him because they know His voice, and they will not follow another. Imagine Jesus the Shepherd sitting beneath a tree with a little lamb in His lap. He is petting and loving the lamb, talking soothingly to it. The lamb could not be happier. Jesus wants us to know we are loved like that.

My grandchildren's little dog Bambi is always being petted and loved. They put their heads on the dog's head and speak affectionate words to her. Once when I invited Bambi to sit on a chair next to me, she looked at one of the kids and decided not to comply. She did not heed my voice. I was not her master.

The word "discern" is defined as the ability to judge well. In a biblical context it means to obtain spiritual direction and understanding; to identify; to tell the difference between things. When Solomon became king, he asked God for **"an understanding heart to judge Your people, that I may discern between good and evil"** (I Kings 3:9 NKJV).

Randy and I have lost money, made many mistakes, and have even gotten into trouble because we lacked discernment. We all need it every day, for every situation. One time when I told a friend we needed to pray for her discernment, she protested, "I don't want discernment because I am an encourager!" To encourage someone appropriately, discernment is essential.

When praying for people, I used to think that discernment was identifying the problem. Instead, it is recognizing its source. Several times, as I was trying to help people, I was hearing my own voice and trying to control them. The Lord said to me, **"Get out of My way."** I was actually harming others by keeping them from God's compassionate correction.

Sometimes, what we think of as discernment can be controlling, which is a form of witchcraft. God delights in directing us and telling us what to do so we can help others, not manipulate them.

Once when I was trying to "fix" somebody, the Lord told me that person was His servant, not mine. Now I try to discern what God is doing in other people's lives, and I realize that I am not their savior.

Misplaced compassion gets in the way of discernment. We can interfere with what God desires to do in someone's life. When sympathy wanted me to help a homeless person who was living in a tent, I asked the Lord about it. He said that person had to learn through suffering. And because I didn't rescue him, he ended up in a wonderful shelter where he was well cared for, and he began to humble himself.

Randy had a dream that he was in a combat unit assigned to go around a mountain and capture a village. Along the way, they encountered people with needs. One place they passed had no source for safe drinking water. Another needed medical assistance and supplies. But the unit had to press on and complete their assignment.

As it turned out, capturing that village was essential to winning a battle and gaining a strategic advantage over the enemy. It was essential to follow orders. The unit could have stopped to do good deeds, gotten sidetracked, and failed to accomplish their mission, enabling the enemy to occupy the entire region. This is how important it is to know your assignment and do it.

We are to ask for God's help to "do the work." When health issues threatened my ability to accomplish a project, God instructed me to "find ways to do what you want to do."

I wanted to paint our deck, so I got an extra long paint brush, sat in my wheelchair with paint clothes on, and painted the whole deck. It turned out great, although I did get paint all over my wheelchair. So we reupholstered the arms and painted black over the paint I got on the rest of it. I had fun.

God will help us find a way to do what He wants us to do, if we ask Him. A religious spirit will try to prevent us from discerning God's voice and recognizing His will.

The Bible is a Christian's operating manual. People are always wanting to know God's will for their lives. If they would read His Word, they would know His will.

25

If you take a portion of the Truth and make it the whole Truth, it becomes not the Truth.

"Pilate said to Him, 'What is truth?'"
(John 18:38 NKJV).

By Randy

"What is truth?" might have been a rhetorical question for Pontius Pilate, but truth has always been the subject of conjecture. Many people base their interpretation of truth on "facts"; however, one man's facts may not be another's. Facts are subject to interpretation.

Many people believe the same way about truth. They think it is relative, and what is true for one person may not be true for another.

Jesus said, **"If you abide in My Word, you are My disciples indeed. And you shall know the Truth, and the Truth shall make you free"** (John 8:31-32 NKJV). He was not talking about truths but the Truth of God. More and more, people scoff at the idea of Absolute Truth and Eternal Truth.

This has not always been the case. At one time it was mandatory when giving testimony in a court of law to put one's hand on a Bible and take an oath to tell "the truth, the whole truth and nothing but the truth, so help me God." Now witnesses can ask to use any other book they consider sacred or no book at all, and "so help me God" is no longer part of being sworn in.

As part of my morning devotions, God has given me this declaration to make: **"I perceive that reality is not what my senses detect; reality is the unshakable Truth of God's Word."**

My father was an aeronautical engineer. To explain the importance of accuracy, he used the illustration of a moon launch. If the rocket is just one degree off course at the beginning, and it is not corrected in flight, it can totally miss its destination.

Like the "little leaven that leavens the whole lump" (Galatians 5:9), so a little bit of error corrupts the whole concept. That is why it is so important to quote Scripture accurately. Misquoting it or applying it out of context can skew the meaning.

The Lord said to me once, **"If you take a portion of the Truth and make it the whole Truth, it becomes not the Truth."**

That is why Paul instructed Timothy, **"Be diligent to present yourself approved to God, a worker who does not need to be ashamed, rightly dividing the Word of Truth"** (II Timothy 2:15 NKJV). "Rightly dividing" means correctly handling and skillfully teaching.

25

So what *is* Truth? The Lord has given Barbara and me many insights in response to that question:

"If there is one Truth that supersedes all truths, what is it? 'God is love.'

"Although that is a simple sentence, it is packed. First, it acknowledges Me. Then it makes Me relevant by saying I AM. Then it summarizes My character in one word – love.

"Don't feel like you have to prove it. Be the truth.

"Whatever twists a truth into condemnation makes it no longer true. In Me, mercy and truth always flow together. Where either one is absent, so is the other."

Sometimes we are tempted to judge truth by whose mouth it comes out of. The Lord clarified:

"Truth does not depend on the vessel; it stands on its own. Truth does not come from a vessel; it comes from Me.

"If I choose to use a flawed vessel, what concern is that of yours? Your job is not to judge the vessel but to discern the Truth. So when someone speaks in My name, take your eyes off the person. Open your ears to what is being said and use the discernment I have given you to know if it is the Truth."

And another time He said:

"Truth glorifies no man, not even he who knows it. Truth only glorifies the Father and the Son and the Holy Spirit, from Whom it emanates.

"To a man who properly handles the Truth, that ability is humbling and not egotistical. He knows the Truth did not come from him but was sent to him as a blessing, and he is responsible to bless others by revealing it to them.

"Neither can a man take it personally when that Truth is not received. He knows he has blessed others with it whether they listen or not. Because that Truth is not his, the people who reject it are not rejecting him but the One who gave the Truth to him in the first place.

"This is how a worker in My vineyards must believe to be effective."

26

What does My Word mean when it says, "Owe no one anything but to love him"?

"For the laborer is worthy of his wages" (Luke 10:7 NKJV).

By Randy

Early in my walk with the Lord, He asked me, **"What does My Word mean when it says, 'Owe no one anything but to love Him'?"**

It was a reference to Paul's instruction in Romans 13:8 (NKJV), **"Owe no one anything except to love one another, for he who loves another has fulfilled the Law."** But at the time, I didn't know that so I answered the best I could. I replied, "It means to pay your bills on time and not to charge up your credit cards."

"It also means no one owes you anything but to love you, too!" the Lord retorted emphatically.

I had entered ministry within a year of becoming a Christian, and it went to my head. I believed I was finally doing something right in my life. I was proud of myself. I was full of myself.

I knew God was calling me to use my training as a journalist to start a Christian newspaper. It was a sacrificial ministry. At first, I was the entire staff. I planned, wrote, edited, proofread, produced and delivered each monthly edition. Plus I sold the advertising. I didn't feel sorry for myself because I was doing what I enjoyed most. But I did have an inflated ego and thought I was being "poured out like a drink offering," as the Bible says.

It was my decision to pursue this ministry at the expense of spending time with my family. I invested my creativity, emotions, resources and identity in it. I thought I was doing it as unto God; but truth be told, I was doing it for my own fulfillment too. So I couldn't blame the ministry for what I was sacrificing.

I could see that other people in my profession, with the same amount of experience, were earning much larger salaries than I did. But that was okay. I was doing this as unto the Lord, not to make money. Still, envy produced a sense of entitlement. I thought people owed me.

I developed the attitude that they should recognize my sacrifice and favor me financially. Whether I was purchasing a product or a service, I thought I deserved special consideration. Whenever I went into a business, I expected people to sell me things for less because they knew I was in ministry. When

I had expenses like car repairs, I thought I should get a discount. After all, I was sacrificing myself for the sake of other people, wasn't I?

That sense of entitlement was also the result of feeling chosen. I thought I was God's gift to the Body of Christ, and that He would use me to bring salvation to all those around me who did not know the Lord. Now I recognize that being a gift means for me to be humble toward others and prefer them in our dealings, not the other way around.

I had a lot to learn about trusting the Lord. I didn't understand yet that if He gave me an assignment, He would be the Source for what I need to complete it, including provision and time for my family. But I was insecure in my beliefs and my way of handling relationships.

When the Lord asked me that question, He was not just disciplining my thinking. He was stimulating my faith. He was saying to expect provision from Him and not other people.

I think back to my attitude of entitlement and I cringe at how I came across. It must have seemed very self-centered and arrogant. And I was supposed to be an ambassador for God's Kingdom!

Years afterward, the Lord gave me this instruction:

"Until a person is secure in his relationship with Me, he will not be secure in other relationships. A man's relationship with Me is a model for his relationships with others. And godly relationships with others are a witness to unbelievers.

"How can anyone who is not secure in Me find fulfillment in a friendship or a marriage? If someone won't come to Me, he looks to appease his emptiness with another person. When that person lets him down, then comes disappointment and bitterness.

"The person who is secure in Me has such an abundance of every godly attribute that, even in his relationships with ungodly people, he is not disappointed or disapproving.

"I AM the Source of your security. It is the principle of living water: Drink from My well and you will never thirst for acceptance from other men, nor drink the bitter water of disappointment in relationships."

27

Teach us to live in Your abundance.

"Now to Him who is able to [carry out His purpose and] do superabundantly more than all that we dare ask or think [infinitely beyond our greatest prayers, hopes, or dreams], according to His power that is at work within us, to Him be the glory" (Ephesians 3:20-21 AMP).

By Barbara

When ministries depend on raising support as their source, they can end up imitating the world's way of doing things. It is a temptation to cross over into manipulation, which is actually witchcraft.

The Lord instructed Randy and me to pray, **"Teach us to live in Your abundance,"** so no longer did we look to people as our source, or speaking engagements, or book sales. It is all from Him. It is according to His riches. What freedom, peace and joy to rest in God's provision!

Jesus said to His followers, **"And do not seek what you should eat or what you should drink, nor have an anxious mind. For all these things the nations of the world seek after, and your Father knows that you need these things. But seek the Kingdom of God, and all these things shall be added to you. Do not fear, little flock, for it is your Father's good pleasure to give you the Kingdom"** (Luke 12:29-32 NKJV)..

Like many people, Randy and I once counted on man for provision when God has all resources. **"The earth is the Lord's, and all its fullness, the world and those who dwell therein"** (Psalm 24:1 NKJV).

One year, our ministry was promised at least $25,000 by various people, and we were not even seeking after it. We never saw a penny. It was an example of what Proverbs 20:25 warns against: **"It is a snare for a man to devote rashly something as holy, and afterward to reconsider his vows"** (NKJV).

It makes us sad when people sabotage themselves like this. It is lying not only to man but to God. We were told that these same people do this to many ministries. It is a man-pleasing spirit. Ananias and Sapphira dropped dead (Acts 5) because of that spirit.

Jesus said, **"Let your 'Yes' be 'Yes,' and your 'No,' 'No.' For whatever is more than these is from the evil one"** (Matthew 5:37 NKJV).

James said, **"Let your 'Yes' be 'Yes,' and your 'No,' 'No,' lest you fall into judgment"** (James 5:12 NKJV).

When God inspires people to give, they become like the children of Israel who gave so much toward the building of the tabernacle that Moses had to tell them to stop (Exodus 36:6). We prefer that way of provision rather than asking people to give. When we take up offerings at our meetings, everything we collect goes to the speaker. We hold back nothing for Shiloh Ministries or ourselves.

We published our first book in 2013. Randy and I agreed to offer it for a voluntary donation or for free, rather than sell it to try to make a profit. Randy knew that people who self-publish to make money are universally disappointed. After prayerfully considering our options, he concluded that the wisest course was to consider the printing expenses as an investment in the Kingdom of God, and to make Him our Source and Provider.

As I was walking in a shopping mall, a man ran up to me from a small kiosk and started buffing my nails with a sparkling, new fingernail file. When he was finished, my nails were all bright and shiny. Since I am an artist, I don't use nail polish because so often, I have paint on my hands. So with my glossy fingernails, I thought, "That is great!" And I said silently, "Oh God, I want one of those."

Before the salesman told me the cost, I knew this product was very expensive, so I stopped at a dollar store and a drug store to look for a cheap alternative. Nothing like it was sold there.

The next day, three women randomly visited me, one after another. I showed them my shiny fingernails and told them my experience. Each one said, "Oh, I have one of those but I never use it," and offered it to me. The last woman said she had two of them, so I asked her for one. I was thrilled.

Years later, I find they do have cheap ones for $3 at the drug store., and they work just as well. But back then, they were $60.

The Lord told us, "There is ample supply in the Body of Christ," and He will make it available to us if we ask Him.

If we all would live out of God's abundance, there would be ample supply for every church, every ministry, every minister, every family, and every individual. There is no shortage with God. There is ample supply.

"And my God shall supply all your need according to His riches in glory by Christ Jesus" (Philippians 4:19 NKJV).

Even a fingernail file.

28

You can't draw water from an empty well.

"If any of you lacks wisdom, let him ask of God, who gives to all liberally and without reproach, and it will be given to him"
(James 1:5 NKJV).

By Randy

When the Lord said to me, "You can't draw water from an empty well," He was telling me several things at once. First and foremost, He was talking about matters of faith and wisdom.

Barbara has always been outspoken about her faith. After I married her, I often found myself in situations where I needed to share my own beliefs – many times with people who were looking to me for answers. I learned quickly that I not only discredited the messenger but my message if I seemed unsure of myself or said something shallow. I needed wisdom.

As I matured in my relationship with the Lord, I found wisdom to be the most satisfying of all the things I could ask Him for. Wisdom was the water I wanted to draw from my well. It has many companions. One of them is favor.

My profession as a journalist charted the course of my Christian walk. The pastor who married Barbara and me previously managed the area's Christian radio station. When he learned I had been a reporter for our county weekly newspaper, it piqued his attention.

He told me, "When I was at the station, I wanted to start a Christian newspaper, but the Lord would not let me. He said He would send someone else to do that. Maybe it's you." I told the pastor I wasn't interested.

When I had responded to an altar call a few weeks earlier, I told God I belonged to Him, and if He could use me for anything, I would do it. And now I was refusing to consider the first thing He asked.

Regardless, something stirred in me. It felt like a big, oriental gong was sounded in my chest. In the weeks to come, I couldn't get that calling out of my mind. It became clear that I was made for this ministry.

Barbara had been an active volunteer and contributor to the Christian station, so they knew her. I submitted a proposal to transform their donor newsletter into a regional Christian publication.

The board of directors requested that I attend a meeting so they could interview me. I was so new as a Christian that they knew nothing about me, so they asked a lot of questions. I shared my testimony and told them I had married Barbara. Then the chairman said, "Well why didn't you say so in the first place?" It was the favor of God. Barbara was the water in my well.

They gave me the green light, and that started an outreach which lasted almost three decades.

Several years later, I came across a back issue of that donor newsletter from the very month I came under conviction to give my life to Christ. An appeal said the station was looking for someone to convert their newsletter into a community publication. I had no idea they were even looking for an editor. That confirmed my belief that it was God's destiny for me.

I learned a lot from that newspaper ministry. Sometimes, when writing a personal testimony or reporting on an event, I was tempted to exaggerate or embellish to "help God look good." I had seen this done in other publications. But I realized that He did not need that kind of help. Plus, if my credibility were compromised even in a small respect, the entire ministry would come into question.

I also recognized that differences of opinion from readers were really a ministry opportunity. Unfortunately, in Christianity, it's hard for everyone to agree on some things. And feedback can be more often negative than positive. Working for a Christian radio station taught me now readily people would find fault with the music we played or a teaching program we aired.

When some articles I printed drew criticism, rather than defend them or take offense, I came to see it as an open door for ministry to the people who complained. Many times, they misunderstood something. By caring about them as a shepherd would, I could identify the source of their problem and offer a perspective which helped them. It was gratifying to turn a negative experience into a positive one.

Then there were those rare times when I had to correct someone in authority, like a pastor. When it would have been easier for me to ignore the situation, I knew caring for their souls was more important than whether I might be rejected. That requires wisdom.

The Living Bible translates James 1:5 this way—

"If you want to know what God wants you to do, ask Him, and He will gladly tell you, for He is always ready to give a bountiful supply of wisdom to all who ask Him. . . ."

29

Be God-confident, not self-conscious.

"Through faith in Him we may approach God with freedom and confidence" (Ephesians 3:12 NIV).

By Randy

All of us who are followers of Jesus Christ are God-confident. Or are we?

Our faith revolves around the atoning sacrifice of Jesus for remission of the world's sin, and the coming Kingdom of God. We put our confidence in Him and the promises found in His Word.

It's easy, however, to relegate Christianity to just another belief system rather than view it as life itself, if our trust in God is not borne out in our everyday decisions.

Often, it's little things that test us. Big things can seem so far out of reach that we feel helpless except for the power of prayer, so we commit them to the Omnipotent God of the Universe. But the routine issues of life tempt us to try to control them on our own. Controlling is manipulation, which is a form of witchcraft and the fruit of vanity.

Self-consciousness is also a trap of vanity. It boils down to being more concerned about what other people think of us than what God thinks of us. We can be self-conscious about our appearance, but more subtle is when we are self-conscious about our performance. None of us likes to fail.

The Lord addressed that when speaking to Barbara and me:

"I can build empires out of your failures. I can use everything you do right and everything you do wrong. When you trust Me that much, then it's about Me and not about you.

"Guilt is about you. Grace is about Me. Be God-confident, not self-conscious. Then it's about Me and not about you."

When Barbara and I were still newlyweds, a friend with a prison ministry asked me to collect cans for a food drive for families of incarcerated men. In my vanity, I thought such a simple task was beneath me, so I gave it a half-hearted try and ended up with seven cans. I was embarrassed by the outcome. Afterward, Barbara asked, "Why didn't you just buy some cans and donate them?" It made sense, but I didn't think of it.

That campaign was for Thanksgiving. At Christmastime, our friend asked me to do it again. I felt exonerated. I was getting a second chance, so I took it seriously and had at it.

29

I discovered that area churches with food banks could not spare anything due to the holidays, and supermarkets only had small quantities of dented cans to donate. After giving it my best, I had collected only seven cans, the same number as before. Once again, I thought I was a failure.

I apologized to the Lord, who assured me He was looking at my attitude and not my performance, and the second time He was pleased with me.

Another of the things the Lord taught us about being God-confident has to do with harvesting souls:

"There are fish in the sea waiting to jump into your net. Will you continue to cast it, or quit when all you haul in are fish which must be thrown back?

"When I told the disciples where to cast their net, the catch was so big that the net was tearing (Luke 5:6). The disciples needed to hear their Master's voice, not just to be obedient but to be confident. Rather than relying on your own strength, everyone who casts a net and is confident in Me will catch fish.

"Why must a fish be thrown back? One of two reasons: Either it is not edible or it is not yet big enough. If you caught a school of baby fish which would yield very little food because they were so small, they would not be worth the trouble to clean. Wouldn't you throw them back and hope to catch them again when they are big enough to be profitable?

"Don't ask, 'Why aren't there many keepers in my net?' Ask instead, 'Am I in the right waters to catch good fish?' If you think you are, then when conditions are right, your net will be full and very few fish will have to be thrown back. You can help the conditions be right by praying."

When we are disturbed at how something turns out or what someone else may think, the Lord desires from us the sacrifice of trusting Him.

"Be angry, yet do not sin. Think about this when upon your beds, and be silent. Offer sacrifices that are righteous, and put your confidence in the Lord" (Psalm 4:4-5 ISV).

"God is our refuge and strength, a very present help in trouble" (Psalm 46:1 NKJV).

30

A good testimony always includes being humbled.

"Humble yourselves in the sight of the Lord, and He will lift you up" (James 4:10 NKJV).

By Barbara

In the 25 years Randy edited the *Manna* newspaper, we printed hundreds of personal testimonies from all kinds of people. Most of them had one thing in common. It seemed to form a pattern.

These people were going through life until a major concern or crisis intervened. Then in desperation they called out to God for help, and He met them at their place of faith. That is what the Bible calls humbling ourselves.

The Lord told us, "A good testimony always includes being humbled."

In James 4;6 and I Peter 5:5 (NKJV), the Bible says, **"God resists the proud, but gives grace to the humble."** James 4:10 says, **"Humble yourselves in the sight of the Lord, and He will lift you up"** (NKJV).

The Lord told us that humility – being willing to overlook offenses – is an important factor that ushers in revival:

"Look at how much Jesus had to suffer just to make a point. It wasn't only what He endured on the cross – it was the grief in His heart every time He tried to gather Our children together, and they were unwilling. It was His anger over injustice when the religious leaders used their position for greed instead of grace. Yet His suffering was due to love and not offense.

"Don't just promote revival, teach that it takes endurance to be prepared for it. The unity which precedes revival cannot exist where there is offense. Offense cannot take place when people give up their right to be offended. That's the fruit of humbling yourselves. Unity is part of the grace I give to the humble."

And about grace, He added:

"Grace is something you receive, and then it is something you walk in. It is salvation. It is growing in your faith. It is made mature and complete as a result of trials. Grace is not just coming to Me but going on with Me."

We have a choice. Either we can humble ourselves, or life will humble us. It's better to pray ahead of a crisis rather than wait to pray until one arrives.

The Lord has proven over and over again something He told us many years ago: "Every question in life and every problem can be overcome by wisdom and humility."

30

Overcoming is part of what we are here to learn. The Lord taught us:

"Satan can take somebody out in one fell swoop if his victim is exceptionally careless. Usually Satan takes people out in slow motion through a process of getting them to agree with him.

"Being an overcomer means not listening to the lies of the enemy but choosing to stand on My Truth in the face of circumstances and feelings. When self-pity becomes a familiar refuge, it will try to drag other fears in with it. So when you're afraid for yourself, soon you're afraid for your family and your ministry. This is how fear spreads like crabgrass.

"You can break loose from fear anytime, but you must want to do it or it won't work. Mumbling scriptures by rote and waiting for Me to move doesn't work. When you stand on My Word, it means you trust it to be ample footing which will support your weight no matter how burdened you are."

He continued::

"Problems are not circumstances. Problems are how you perceive circumstances. People you know who don't seem to have many problems still encounter adversity. People with lots of problems struggle with circumstances which may not be that much worse than a happy person's.

"It is true that people who perceive problems attract problems. But their problem is not their circumstances, it is their outlook. Likewise, the optimist and the joy-filled believer and the faithful servant all see their adverse circumstances as an opportunity for overcoming, rather than an injury or insult.

"Many so-called problems are the result of human actions, not an attack from Satan nor a test from Me. That's why the person who feels sorry for himself will always have more reasons to feel sorry for himself. The one who lives in fear will always have more to fear. And the one who seeks to be free in Me will one day be free indeed."

31

Everything is preparation.

"It has not yet been revealed what we shall be, but we know that when He is revealed, we shall be like Him"

(I John 3:2 NKJV)

By Randy

When the Lord said to Barbara and me, "Everything is preparation," it gave us a greater understanding of the connection between our actions and experiences in the present, and what to expect in the future.

It is the principle of sowing and reaping: **"Do not be deceived, God is not mocked; for whatever a man sows, that he will also reap. For he who sows to his flesh will of the flesh reap corruption, but he who sows to the Spirit will of the Spirit reap everlasting life"** (Galatians 6:7-8 NKJV).

This life is a rehearsal – preparation for eternity. Everything we do now contributes to what lies ahead. Our daily activities have lasting meaning.

I like being prepared; it's a form of security… and control. When I started a journalism career at age 18, I found one of its most intimidating requirements was speaking over the phone. I feared I was too young to be taken seriously, that I had no influence, and that I couldn't get what I was calling for. But I discovered my voice had favor. Good phone presence was a helpful tool. Sometimes I could persuade people by phone more than in person.

I started rehearsing my words ahead of time to achieve optimum results. Coming to the point quickly was most effective. I carefully scripted myself, planning each word I would say. By phrasing my questions just right, I could not only get what I wanted out of people, but they enjoyed talking with me.

It worked so well that I used the same technique for other activities, and eventually I was rehearsing everything important. I rehearsed life itself so I could make outcomes go my way.

This habit continued into my later years. I learned that rehearsing was a way to get people to do what I wanted without incurring their resentment. I considered rehearsing a sophisticated form of preparation until the Lord told me to "stop rehearsing the future." I needed to let Him be in charge.

I have had to learn the difference between viewing my experiences as preparation, and rehearsing life as an method to manipulate it.

What is the ultimate objective of our preparation? Becoming more like Jesus.

31

The life of Joseph is an example of how everything is preparation. Each event paved the way for what was to come, not only for him but for the generations which followed.

Joseph was his father Jacob's favorite child. His renowned coat of many colors was a gift from Jacob which set Joseph above His siblings, sparking bitter jealousy among his 11 brothers.

They hated him all the more when Joseph related his night vision of them all bowing down to him, acknowledging his authority over them. His brothers derisively called him "this dreamer."

An ideal opportunity to get rid of Joseph arose when he was sent to check on his brothers' well-being. They were angry enough to murder him, but instead they greedily sold him to a passing caravan which carried Joseph to Egypt as a slave. There he was sold to Potiphar, the captain of Pharaoh's guard.

God prospered everything entrusted to Joseph, so Potiphar appointed him over his entire household. When Potiphar's wife repeatedly tried to seduce Joseph and he refused, she accused him of attempting to rape her and he was sent to prison.

The keeper of the prison also perceived God's favor on Joseph and put him in charge of the other prisoners. When two of Pharoah's servants were sent to the prison and had troubling dreams, Joseph used his gift of interpretation to explain the dreams to them. This brought him to Pharaoh's attention when Pharaoh dreamed that seven years of abundance would be followed by seven years of scarcity. Recognizing Joseph's capacity for stewardship, Pharaoh made him second in command of all Egypt. Joseph organized a system for storing food while there was abundance, so the people would not starve when famine came.

Famine affected the entire world. Jacob heard there was food in Egypt, so he sent Joseph's brothers to buy some. Joseph was in charge, and they bowed before him. They had to buy food from their long-lost brother. That was when Joseph said, **"God sent me before you to preserve a posterity for you in the earth, and to save your lives by a great deliverance"** (Genesis 45:7 NKJV). So Joseph saved not only his brothers and father, but ensured the posterity of his people.

It is easy to see how each event in Joseph's life, no matter how distasteful or unfair at the time, was preparation and part of God's larger plan.

32

Do you really believe that? Do you believe that enough to do it?

"Don't just listen to God's Word. You must do what it says. Otherwise, you are only fooling yourselves" (James 1:22 NLT).

By Randy

The Bible says, **"the testing of your faith produces patience"** (James 1:3 NKJV). My faith was severely tested several years ago when we had a huge financial challenge.

We had taken out a home equity line of credit to help our son buy a house and to absorb a few other expenses. Unwisely, we paid only interest on the loan and let it roll over every five years. After I was no longer working and we were living on Social Security, the bank said we had to reapply for the loan. The problem was, we didn't earn enough money to qualify for it, so it matured into a mortgage and we had to start paying off the principle.

Our payments more than tripled. They were two-thirds of our monthly income. How were we going to go on? It looked like we could lose our house.

Barbara was upbeat and faith-filled, but I was worried sick and depressed. I couldn't sleep. I lost lots of weight. I had withdrawn into survival mode, trying to anticipate all the negative possibilities: If we lost the house, where would we move? How could we accomplish the Herculean task of downsizing? Would home-based Shiloh Ministries be able to continue?

I called the bank to see if I could renegotiate the mortgage. Customer service kept sending me to the sales department to reapply. I was going around in circles.

After two applications for restructuring the loan were denied, I was about to give up. But something told me to call one more time. It was a Friday at 4 p.m. My call was taken by a manager in customer service who really wanted to help us, and personally handled our appeal. She was able to decrease the payments to something we could afford, plus she lowered the interest rate and made it fixed instead of variable. If I had waited until Monday, we would not have been allowed to reapply for another year.

During this process, I had to make some firm commitments to my faith and declare what I believed in. But this was just the beginning. One morning as I was preparing for my day, the Lord brought to mind a principle I had written about in the newspaper or taught somewhere. Then He asked me, **"Do you really believe that?"** It was the beginning of 18 months of daily pop quizzes from Him.

32

He asked if I really believed in the sanctity of life. That marriage is a sacred oath between a man and a woman. That there is absolute Truth. That we are to pray for all those in authority whether we agree with them of not. Every day, it was another question.

At first I thought He was upbraiding me for some lack of commitment. Each morning there was a new reminder of something on which I had taken a stand, followed by the same question, "Do you really believe that?" But these were not tests to call my faith into question. I could tell they were intended to make me think about my personal convictions and declare them. It was a method of building my faith. It was the power of confession. When I confessed my beliefs, I was giving power to my convictions.

As this pattern continued over the months, it did not weary me but it encouraged me. I felt God's love. It was not a religious exercise, it was forcing me to come into agreement with myself. I sensed strength from it. I was able to sleep well. My appetite returned. As my spirit man went, so went the rest of me.

I was getting used to this morning faith-builder. Then, one day, the procedure changed. The Lord continued to remind me of things I stood for, then He asked, "Do you believe that enough to do it?" This put it in a different perspective. I was not only being called to declare what I believed but to live it.

Some scriptures started impacting me on a deeper level:

"But be doers of the word, and not hearers only, deceiving yourselves" (James 1:22 NKJV).

"For the Kingdom of God is not based on talk but on power" (I Corinthians 4:20 AMP).

"If you love Me, keep My commandments" (John 14:15 NKJV).

The Lord wanted me to understand that, even in His Kingdom, talk is cheap. I had gone through a classic example of a problem being an opportunity in work clothes.

The Lord taught me to pray, "I take authority over our finances. I declare we have entered our season of increase, redemption, restitution, restoration and abundance, and I ask God to continue bringing it to pass."

33

You don't drink the water that primes the pump.

"Better is the end of a thing than its beginning; and the patient in spirit is better than the proud in spirit"

(Ecclesiastes 7:8 RSV).

By Barbara

When we started Shiloh Ministries, we thought it was going to be an outreach to single mothers. I raised my family alone for almost 10 years before Randy and I were married, and I didn't want others to suffer the way I did. A ministry to single moms seemed like a natural fit for me.

We spent months planning it. We would operate a large retail store, containing a factory where customers could watch the women hand paint furniture and make Scripture banners to generate income. The store would also contain a tea room/restaurant, and provide a consignment area for other ministries to display things for sale. We would buy houses to have places for these moms and their kids to live.

There was only one problem. Every time we talked about it, we both felt nauseated. But we did not want to disobey the vision, and we pursued it.

People donated all sorts of stuff. Two Christian bookstores that went out of business gave us displays and the merchandise they couldn't sell. We stored all this in the barn behind our house, cramming it from floor to ceiling on two levels with donations for our store. A friend anonymously contributed $5,000 to get us started.

We thought we needed a director because we were so unsure of ourselves, so we hired a woman from the Midwest who had a lot of experience operating large ministries. We believed this was of God.

We assembled a board, started holding planning meetings, and laid out a five-year strategy. Our director required a salary of $500 a week, and said she needed a secretary, whom we hired for an additional $400 a week.

Shiloh had no way to produce income yet, so I worked nonstop making banners and painting business signs to help pay the salaries. Still, things deteriorated rapidly. Our fundraisers lost money. Once, we set up a booth to make sandwiches at a beach appreciation day, only to have a nor'easter roar through the night before. Only a handful of people attended, and we were stuck with nearly the entire $1,000 of food my daughter donated.

Our director moved back to the Midwest just before the final fundraiser. The secretary disappeared. The volunteers evaporated. Only Randy and I were left. We invested $40 for ingredients and baked several hundred brownies to sell at a town fair, and made $10.

33

In three months we went through the entire $5,000 plus another $3,000 of my hard-earned income. Even with our good intentions, we failed.

I was devastated and stayed mad at God and everyone else for a month. As I dealt with the humiliation of telling people our big plans, then spending all our funds to accomplish nothing, I finally asked God what happened. "You learned your lesson cheap," He replied.

"What lesson?"

Then He said, "You sold your birthright."

Because He gave *us* the calling, the anointing was on *us* to direct it. Rather than hiring someone, we should have trusted Him to make *us* equal to the task. It was disrespecting God's anointing.

We decided to renovate the barn and make it into the factory where the single moms would work. The building was an empty shell. We ran utilities to it and finished the inside. We named it Redemption Depot.

All that work took nine months and we were eager to start the ministry, so we asked the Lord how to begin. "Have parties," He said.

"WHAT?" We were stunned. That was so far from what we envisioned. But, believing God had a master plan, we complied.

We had all kinds of functions in Redemption Depot, from tea parties to puppet shows to fellowship dinners, every one with a Gospel theme. We made them family friendly. People came from all over. We had more than 1,000 visitors to our property that first year.

Gradually the gatherings shifted to ministry meetings where guest speakers taught on the prophetic and intercession. Redemption Depot was a perfect facility in which to hold them. After seeing what Shiloh Ministries eventually became, we asked the Lord where we missed it at the beginning.

"You don't drink the water that primes the pump," He told us. In the country, when people get their water from outdoors, a little water is reserved to pour down the neck of the hand pump so the gaskets create suction to draw with. You don't drink the water that primes the pump. It was another way of telling us, "You couldn't have gotten to here from where you were."

We would never have understood what He wanted at first, so we had to take this detour to receive His vision for the ministry.

34

Taking the Lord's name in vain is wearing His identity without demonstrating His character.

"Remove falsehood and lies far from me;
give me neither poverty nor riches –
feed me with the food allotted to me;
lest I be full and deny You, and say,
'Who is the Lord?' Or lest I be poor and
steal, and profane the name of my God"
(Proverbs 30:8–9 NKJV).

By Randy

Like many of us, I grew up being told not to take the Lord's name in vain. To me, that meant not to use His name as an expletive.

Those were times when obscene language was not allowed in broadcasting or the movies, nor in public. But that was then, this is now. Today's world has different standards for morals.

I knew better than to take the Lord's name in vain in the classic sense. Now, as a Christian, I realize that I didn't understand the concept completely. Of course it includes using His name as an expletive. But the Lord revealed to me a broader meaning that has much deeper implications:

"Taking the Lord's name in vain is wearing His identity without demonstrating His character."

Christians literally wear the name of Christ. Sometimes we are called "Jesus people." The challenge is not just to be called by His name but to be like Him.

The Bible tells us in many places to demonstrate the character of the Lord. Perhaps the most detailed is Colossians 3:12-15 (CSB):

"Therefore, as God's chosen ones, holy and dearly loved, put on compassion, kindness, humility, gentleness, and patience, bearing with one another and forgiving one another if anyone has a grievance against another. Just as the Lord has forgiven you, so you are also to forgive. Above all, put on love, which is the perfect bond of unity. And let the peace of Christ, to which you were also called in one body, rule your hearts. And be thankful."

Paul instructed, **"Imitate me, just as I also imitate Christ"** (I Corinthians 11:1 NKJV). John wrote, **"Beloved, now we are children of God; and it has not yet been revealed what we shall be, but we know that when He is revealed, we shall be like Him, for we shall see Him as He is"** (I John 3:2 NKJV).

Using the name of Jesus to cuss has become so commonplace that it hardly draws an objection anymore. But when Barbara and I volunteered at The Son'Spot Christian Fellowship Center in Ocean City, we occasionally encountered a person who had never heard the name of Jesus, not even used as an expletive. It's hard to imagine that anyone could grow up in this country and never hear the name of Jesus. Explaining who He is to someone like that is challenging and exciting. It's being a missionary.

We start demonstrating the character of Jesus when we ask Him into our hearts. That's how we find peace as God's children. He told us:

"I want you to understand the full meaning of being My son. You're not *becoming* My son, you *are* My son. It's not something you earn. You don't have to pass a test because you have already asked the key question: You asked Jesus to come into your heart to be your Lord. So now you are a member of My family.

"Children in a family have privileges. You have the privilege of wearing My name and sharing in My riches. Even if you don't see them yet, they are coming to you. They will be more than earthly riches. They will be the deep things of God that have eternal value. They will create understanding and make the way for other people to see clearly how to leave behind the things of this world that entangle them and prevent them from being members of My family.

"You're going to instruct people. You're going to demonstrate how to avoid the things that distract and deceive them, that cause them to doubt and fear. You're going to show people how to have a relationship with Me that is full of joy, and how to have total peace.

"These are times when peace is going to be very, very hard to find. The people who have peace will be like you – people who have come to know Me, who are willing to give up everything for intimacy with Me, who have the assurance that whatever things look like, I AM still there for them. The world wants that. They don't know how to find it. You are going to have the ministry of reconciliation which demonstrates for people that it's possible. You are going to show people the way. This is what I'm raising you up to do.

"You're going to have some time on the back side of the desert, some time of instruction. You're going to be seasoned like firewood. The longer it seasons, the hotter it burns. I want you to be encouraged that you are starting on the good journey of your life.

"When you doubted yourself, you wondered if this were even possible. Now you're learning who you really are, and you're going to become who I made you to be."

35

There is a difference between responding to Me and resting in Me.

"Rest in the Lord, and wait patiently for Him" (Psalm 37:7 NKJV).

By Barbara

I have been conscious of God since I was a little girl. Even before I gave my heart to Jesus, my belief in God was strong, and I wanted to please Him.

That was me responding to God. But He wanted me to do more than be aware of Him – He wanted me to trust Him by resting in Him.

A few years ago, the Lord told me, "There is a difference between responding to Me and resting in Me."

He also said, "What is rest? It is abandoning the need to control. The worries which incite you to control keep you from resting. Resting is not only a matter of physical stillness; it is peace in the inmost being, which comes from trusting Me with all your circumstances."

My artistic, creative nature never lets up. I can enter a room and before I sit down, I have redecorated it in my mind. When colors are wrong, it grieves me. I want to fix things because I want to honor my Creator. I believe beauty does that, so I try to beautify things wherever I can.

Because of this drive to make things pretty, it is hard for me to rest. Sure, I like to get enough sleep. But as the Lord told me, resting is not just physical, it is the measure of how much we trust Him.

The Bible reveals a lot about entering His rest. Hebrews 4:1 (TPT) says, **"Now God has offered to us the same promise of entering into His realm of resting in confident faith. So we must be extremely careful to ensure that we all embrace the fullness of that promise and not fail to experience it."**

Resting is operating in God's strength, rather than trying to please Him in our own strength. It's the difference between faith and works.

When God corrects me, I don't just feel the sting of a rebuke; I feel the reassurance of His love. At the time He said this to me, I was suffering from a severe bout of sciatica:

"I have told you to rest. It was not only to avoid physical pain but to relieve emotional stress. Now I'm going to break you of the big one.

"I challenge your thinking that says, 'Unless I push, nothing happens.' That makes you god of your own world. Even when you pray and acknowledge Me, it is all subordinate to your belief that you must bring everything to pass. Your back is bowed from the weight of taking My place.

"I'm not talking about your planning and preparation. I'm talking about seeing yourself as the trail boss. Don't shrink the room I need to reveal Myself. Don't compete with Me. Don't take credit, even if you never tell anyone.

"It is the stress of being in charge of results that has caused you pain – carrying burdens I never intended for you. When you stop doing this, you will see a multitude of benefits. Pain will abate. Strength will return because you spend your energy wisely. Family relationships will improve. Personal fears will decline dramatically. Peace and joy will take their place.

"Kiss your old life goodbye. You don't need to let it hold you back with hidden resentments. You can no longer be the hero or the victim."

A friend and I were discussing my health issues. She told me that autoimmune disease is from self-hatred, which causes your body to attack itself. She also mentioned that our cells have brains (cell memory).

In my imagination I saw tiny round white cells wearing little brains like hats. Recognizing that this had been an open door to sickness, I asked the Lord where self-hatred in me came from. He said, "Other people talked you into it."

I immediately thought back to elementary school, when I was called "Monkey Arms" because I had hairy arms. Later, people called me stupid. A teacher called me "Sleepy." I wonder how many other words were spoken to make me doubt my worth.

Even after I became a Christian, people rolled their eyes and made fun of my attempts to be obedient. Every one of us has been bullied, and ultimately it all comes from our accuser, the devil, using other people.

Many of us internalized these taunts, which handicapped us. This made me realize that God is My Creator, and everything He made is perfect, even with my perceived flaws. These were given to me for overcoming.

I repented for disrespecting the creation God made me. He designed me for His purpose, flaws and all. I determined to start loving myself. Then in my imagination, I saw my little cells dancing around and saying, "She finally got it!"

36

Don't compare.

"For we dare not class ourselves or compare ourselves with those who commend themselves. But they, measuring themselves by themselves, and comparing themselves among themselves, are not wise"

II Corinthians 10:12 (NKJV).

By Randy

As a baby Christian, I was very self-conscious around Barbara's friends. Most of them were mature believers, and I knew almost nothing about the faith I had confessed at an altar call.

I enjoyed my status as the new kid on the block. It was like being a celebrity. People liked talking with me and I basked in the attention.

My life was starting all over again. Some of the people I was meeting had been Christians for decades. I wasn't jealous, but I found myself doing a lot of comparing.

Eventually the Lord had to instruct me, "Don't compare." He showed me that when we compare, we don't come out even. Either we feel superior, which is pride; or we feel inferior, which is envy.

Comparing is not just a pitfall for new Christians. It tempts us all. In my case, it came from the insecurity of an orphan spirit.

Years later, when I was no longer a novelty, I had to deal with that orphan spirit. The Lord gave me some pointers:

"Stop thinking about what you aren't. After all, I'm in charge of what you are and are not. Worrying about what you lack is envy that comes from an orphan spirit.

"Think about what you are. By that I mean, first, be grateful. Second, be content. And third, trust Me that if you need more, I will supply it.

"Gratitude is healing for the orphan spirit."

Now that I, too, have been a Christian for decades, I've had time to recognize the danger of yielding to envy. There are many references to it in Scripture. The first chapter of Romans includes envy in a list of characteristics of ungodly men who **"did not like to retain God in their knowledge."** (vs. 28 NKJV). Some other passages are:

Proverbs 14:30 (NKJV)—**"A sound heart is life to the body, but envy is rottenness to the bones."**

Romans 13:13 (NKJV)—**"Let us walk properly, as in the day, not in revelry and drunkenness, not in lewdness and lust, not in strife and envy."**

36

It was because of envy that the religious leaders handed Jesus over to the Romans to be crucified; and for the same reason, the Jews persecuted Paul.

James wrote, **"For where there is envy and selfish ambition, there is disorder and every evil practice."** (3:16 CSB).

Envy comes from comparing. The Lord told Barbara and me:

"How many times have I told you not to compare? Why do you suppose that is? You are right to say, 'So I won't envy or feel sorry for myself.' But there is another reason why you should not compare – because I do not compare.

"When My Word says I AM no respecter of persons, it means this: When I look into your heart, I do not judge your performance against that of other people. Actually, there is really only one act you can perform to please Me – have faith. That's why I don't look at the outer man. I look in the heart to see if you have received My Love, My Son."

Sometimes we compare ourselves to an imaginary standard. It seldom builds our faith or makes us more confident in God. Doing this only causes us to feel bad about ourselves. It takes our eyes off what God says about us and multiplies our insecurities.

We can also envy other people's God-given talents and spiritual gifts. Most of the time, talents and gifts come at a cost and we pay a personal price for possessing them. Someone who envies these qualities usually wants them free for the asking, and does not want to experience the inconvenience or sacrifice they may require.

Perhaps the most admired of these gifts is soul-winning, which cannot be done selfishly. The Lord explained to us:

"If you want to be a soul-winner, you must learn to think about others and not yourself. It doesn't just mean to stop complaining, it means that you will have nothing to complain about. It also means you will point the way to Me and not be the way.

"In order not to get puffed up by the power of being a harvester, you must first be totally secure in Me. To do that, you must stop looking at other people with eyes of envy, and start looking at them with a heart of compassion."

37

Remove what is dead in me and prune what remains, so I will bear much fruit for Your Kingdom.

"Every branch in Me that does not bear fruit He takes away; and every branch that bears fruit He prunes, that it may bear more fruit" (John 15:2 NKJV).

By Barbara

I was taking back roads on my way to help a church with its interior decor, when I drove past a field where scavengers were feeding on a deer carcass. They looked like buzzards, but when they were startled and flew away, I could see the white heads and tails of the adults. They were bald eagles. The immature ones did not have their markings yet and appeared to be brown.

Eagles represent the prophetic, so I supposed what I saw had a deeper meaning than in the physical realm. The digital clock on the dashboard said 1:11 and I wondered what the significance was.

When I got home, I asked Randy to pray with me about it. The Lord told us it signified **"transition."**

For 10 years, people had been prophesying to us that we were in a period of transition. And we've seen evidence of its fulfillment. During the 25 years that Randy edited the *Manna*, it was a consuming ministry which took up his days and nights. When he was directed to move his office from our home to the studios of the radio station which published it, that began a season of great transition. Eventually he was replaced as editor, reduced to part-time, then dismissed.

We had already started our own ministry by then, so Randy shifted his efforts to Shiloh Ministries, which we operated in our home. In addition to holding house meetings and leading prayer incursions, Shiloh published our first book. The Lord had told us to write it 20 years earlier, and after several false starts, we got serious and finished it in 2013. We were like the barren woman who finally had a child. Once the birth canal was opened, the books just kept tumbling out.

We were definitely in transition. After my sighting of the eagles, we asked the Lord how we should pray. He said to pray this way:

"Lord, guide me through this transition. Remove what is dead in me and prune what remains, so I will bear much fruit for Your Kingdom."

So now, whenever a clock reads 1:11 or any series of identical numbers, it reminds us to pray this transition prayer.

Jesus went through a transition on His way to the cross. Before He was arrested, He met with His disciples for the Passover Supper and washed their feet. Then He told them what was to come. He declared:

"I am the true vine, and My Father is the vinedresser. Every branch in Me that does not bear fruit He takes away; and every branch that bears fruit He prunes, that it may bear more fruit.... I am the vine, you are the branches. He who abides in Me, and I in him, bears much fruit"
(John 15:1-2, 5 NKJV).

Our time of transition is still ongoing. It has been a process. Whenever we don't understand what we are going through or why, we have peace knowing that our Father sees all and has our best interest at heart. He once told us:

"Most things in life are not events but processes that take time. Trust Me through the processes that take time. Don't attach conditions to your trust or create deadlines which are set-ups for discouragement. Real trust is unconditional.

"In the pruning process, you must suffer loss before you bear more fruit. Whenever you suffer loss, it's only temporary on the way to greater abundance."

As we were praying about enduring the process of transition, the Father called the fruit we produce "the joy of unity." He told us:

"Jesus and I are totally One, and no unifying process was necessary because He came from Me.

"Couples come from different backgrounds and form a union. So for them, becoming one is a process of yielding to each other. Included in that process is recognizing gifted areas and learning to trust. That's when the two together are greater than the two separately.

"It's really a process of humility. Those who are willing will find great joy in it."

He also called this "the process of perfection," and described how to view people who seem to suffer loss as they go through it:

"You will recognize what they are reaching for and not gape at what they leave behind. Remember that no man who receives Me can ever be the same again. He is on a path toward righteousness, and that is what I look for."

38

Shorten the season of bad fruit.

"A good tree cannot bear bad fruit, nor can a bad tree bear good fruit" (Matthew 7:18 NKJV).

God's Sayings – *Proverbs, Enigmas & Riddles*

By Randy

The best field training I experienced for introducing others to the Lord was at The Son'Spot Christian Fellowship Center in Ocean City. All kinds of people came in, from operators of the rides and games on the boardwalk to homeless kids who lived in the resort for the summer.

Although some of our guests at The Son'Spot had been to church before, and a few were the children of pastors, most did not have a relationship with God. As they grew to trust us, they would listen as we talked to them about their souls and eternity.

I used to say to them, "Did you know you had an appointment to be here?" Most were surprised, even shocked, and they would say, "No." Then I said, "God wanted you here so He could show you how much He loves you." That took the attention off of me and put it on Him, and the guests were delighted.

In the course of a summer, Barbara and I and the other volunteers led a lot of these visitors in a prayer of salvation, asking God to forgive their sins and Jesus to be the Lord of their lives.

Some of these guests were occasional visitors, but most frequented The Son'Spot throughout the summer. We could observe their spiritual condition and watch the ones who prayed to be saved.

For those whose lives were chaotic when they received the Lord, changes in their circumstances did not happen right away. Some had histories of run-ins with the police. Or they came from troubled homes.

They were usually guarded when they first came in to The Son'Spot. The Christian atmosphere was foreign to them. But once they got used to it, they told us more than we wanted to know.

They would get arrested for a variety of offenses: sleeping in a car overnight, which is illegal in Ocean City; having an open container of alcohol in public; exceeding permitted noise levels at night; and of course, drug possession. Or they lost their job, their girlfriend left, their car stopped running, they were evicted, and a dozen other problems.

Some of them did not have jobs and crashed wherever someone offered them a sofa for the night. They were living day-to-day. I tried to get them to think ahead and have a plan by asking what their ambition was. I received empty looks in return. So I would phrase it differently and ask what was most important to them. The answer I got most often was, "Stay out of jail."

When these unstable kids asked Jesus to be the Lord of their lives, they expected things to change overnight. If their circumstances were not immediately altered, it was easy for them to get discouraged and give up on their commitment to be Christians. I wanted to encourage them to hang in there, so I would ask them to pray this prayer the Lord gave me:

"Father, in Your mercy and grace, I ask You to shorten the season of bad fruit in my life from the bad seeds I have planted, and hasten the season of good fruit from the seeds I am planting now."

We got to know many of our guests personally. Some of them returned every year. Barbara was especially good at remembering their names. In addition to the weekly dinners, she headed up breakfasts four days a week. She made sure to talk to everyone who came, and she made many friends.

Sometimes after partying all night, they would camp out in front of the building and be waiting when she showed up at 6 a.m. to start getting breakfast ready. They didn't want to miss it.

Occasionally after someone made a profession of faith, we saw no difference in their behavior. So we asked the Lord if we were doing something wrong, like making a sinner's prayer too easy. He said to us:

"A sinner goes to the altar and says a prayer of repentance, but you don't see any change in the days afterward. So you conclude that he was insincere, and nothing happened.

"Wrong. He issued an invitation.

"If someone gives Me the legal right to come in, I come in whether he likes it or not. The invitation doesn't have to be sincere, it only needs to be given.

"Insincerity may extend the time before results are seen, but I will not ignore his hospitality. It will take a lot longer for Me to work in the heart of a man who resists Me, but I will do it.

"When men are insincere, they are double-minded. So I wait for them to become more desperate. Love is a good reason for men to come to Me, but desperation will work in a pinch."

39

Whenever you stress, your heart is far from Me.

"Give all your worries and cares to God, for He cares about you" (I Peter 5:7 NLT).

By Barbara

I never lost the hypervigilance I learned when I had small children. I have always been keenly aware of my surroundings, and over time that sensitivity has grown stronger.

As an artist, I am sensitive to colors and textures and what goes together. As a minister, I have learned to be alert to what is going on around me.

When I was on a trip to Israel with a group of intercessors, we were told to be watchful for pickpockets and other thieves who prey on tourists. When I broke off from the main group to go to the Wailing Wall, I was very cautious. My guide was a short Arab Christian named David.

We hurried down the ancient, narrow streets and paused to look around at every corner. Three young Arab men suddenly appeared in front of us. Laughing, they grabbed David and held him over a small fire they had built. They obviously knew him. I was not afraid and shouted, "No! No! No!" Totally surprised at my boldness and command of the situation, they released him and backed up to a wall. David was unharmed and we scurried on.

We retraced our steps on the return trip and encountered those three men once more. As they went to grab David again, I demanded, "No! No! No!" The same thing happened a second time. I was not anxious because I knew God had sent me on that trip, and that He would take care of me.

I must admit, I often have trouble not being anxious and worrying. Many times the Lord has had to remind me not to fear. Once He said to me:

"Satan can't scare you with things that are external to your experience because they are not personal. The world is a scary and dangerous place, but your world isn't. So Satan tries to scare you with fears that the terrible things of the world will invade your world.

"If he can get your attention, he will make your imagination race. Next thing you know, you're dwelling on evil rather than good, and fearing things which are not as though they were.

"If Satan can excite your imagination to dwell on evil, or cause you to fear loss, he can steal your focus, pollute your mind, fracture your love, and extinguish your joy.

39

"When a person is living in fear, his behavior becomes bizarre. He feels persecuted, and in extreme circumstances he could harm others to defend himself against what he irrationally fears.

"Fear is like crabgrass. Satan will start by bringing in fear through familiar things so he can make you afraid of everything and snuff out your faith like a candle."

Fear of actual danger is the mind's defense mechanism for protecting the body. Fear of imagined danger lets the mind be in charge instead of the spirit. As a person with a vivid imagination, that's where I have to be careful.

Fear of lack is where Randy must guard his mind. The Lord told him:

"Fear is anxiety over lack. If you believe I supply all your needs, then you have no fear. Any area where you're tempted to be anxious is where the deceiver has convinced you that you will suffer lack because I will not provide."

The Lord showed Randy and me that many if not most of the things we fear never come to pass. That makes the majority of our fears irrational. To be in an ongoing state of fear is being anxious. He said:

"Every time you're anxious, you're not putting your trust in Me. I know everything you need, whether it's time, money, spiritual or material things.

"Trust Me for all things, even if you must lose some of them. Otherwise, how can you expect to stand in the day when men would take away from you much more than these little things you worry about?

"Whatever imperfect thing you lose in this world will be restored to you many times over in My Kingdom through That Which is Perfect.

"My Word tells you it is preferable to let yourself be defrauded, rather than to take your brother to court. That means it is better to suffer loss than to deny Me by the thoughts of your heart.

"If you feel sorry for yourself, you are telling the whole world you believe I AM not sufficient to meet all your needs.

"When it is necessary to lose something, learn to gladly suffer loss. Or else, how will you keep the testimony of My love and your salvation when the days become more evil? Put material things in perspective. Determine what is truly important and cling to that which is good."

40

I AM the God of unlikely vessels.

"I will have mercy on whomever I will have mercy, and I will have compassion on whomever I will have compassion" (Romans 9:15 NKJV).

By Randy

The power of God can transform an ordinary life into an extraordinary one. The Lord once told Barbara and me He is **"the God of unlikely vessels."**

There was nothing remarkable about my young life. I had been a poor student in school. The label for kids like me was "underachiever." My low opinion of myself preceded me into my adult years.

I had some good jobs after college, but the company I kept was inappropriate. I got involved with druggies and felons. By the time I reached 33 years old, I was unemployed and wondered what happened to my life.

Then I had time to think. The crowd I ran with had unwritten rules: You don't let your friends stay in jail, and you never rat on other people. But I saw those rules broken when the heat was on, and deduced I could not trust anyone.

I had grown up in a home where we did not invest our emotions in one another but in things. Material objects cannot return love; all they can do is get old, require maintenance, and break someday. So I knew I couldn't put my trust in possessions either.

I concluded that I could not even trust myself. Look how I ended up. What was there left to believe in? From the depths of my being came the thought, "The only thing that makes sense is that God is who the Bible says He is." *Where did that come from?*

My logic followed this tangent: "If God is who the Bible says He is, that means that Jesus is who the Bible says He is. And if that's true, He is coming back for the people who are saved." I had heard about "being saved" from the popular culture. I didn't know what it meant, but I knew whatever it was, I wasn't. Unless something changed, I was going to hell.

That *really* scared me. I didn't want to end up in a place I could never get out of, where I would be tormented throughout all eternity.

I knew people had been praying for my salvation. During my years as a retailer, some of my customers shared the Gospel with me. I was polite but not interested. Now the things I disregarded in church as a youth were coming back to me as an adult.

When I tried to read the King James Bible I was given in Sunday school, I couldn't understand it. So I searched for one I could follow. When I got a new Bible, I didn't know where to begin. So I sat it on its binding and let it fall open. Each time it went to the same place – Isaiah 52 - 54. So I figured that was where I was supposed to read. It is a prophetic account of Jesus' Crucifixion, written 700 years before His birth.

It says, **"Many were amazed at Him; for His appearance was marred more than that of any man, and His form more than that of the sons of men.... But He was slain for our sins, He was afflicted for our iniquities; the chastisement of our peace was upon Him, and with His wounds we are healed"** (52:14, 53:5 LAMSA).

When I read the book of John later, those verses kept coming back to my mind, and I felt God's love as I never had before.

I was an unlikely vessel for Him to use, yet He pursued me until I recognized His love for me and could no longer resist it.

Of all the unlikely vessels in Scripture, Gideon is a role model in many ways. He was not a bold man. The invading Midianites returned every year not only to steal Israel's harvest but to destroy it. And they took their herds. It was primitive ethnic cleansing. The Bible says the Midianites were "as numerous as locusts." And they wanted to wipe out Israel.

When the raiders came one year, Gideon was threshing wheat in the winepress so he would not be seen. There, the Angel of the Lord greeted him, **"The Lord is with you, you mighty man of valor!"** (Judges 6:12 NKJV). That statement was prophetic, and there was more. **"Go in this might of yours, and you shall save Israel from the hand of the Midianites. Have I not sent you?"** (vs. 14).

Gideon protested, but he was told, **"Surely I will be with you, and you shall defeat the Midianites as one man.... Peace be with you; do not fear, you shall not die" "** (vss. 16, 23).

After amassing warriors to oppose the Midianites, the Lord told him he had too many people, and reduced their number to 300 to go against an enemy so numerous that they could not be counted. As He promised, God was with them and caused the Midianites to turn on one another, then flee. Gideon pursued them, captured their princes and executed them.

God chose a man whose response to His calling was tantamount to saying, "Who, *me*?" Gideon was an unlikely vessel, and God used him.

41

Make it the desire of your heart so I can give it to you.

"May He grant you according to your heart's desire, and fulfill all your purpose" (Psalm 20:4 NKJV).

By Barbara

I have learned to tell God everything, from my fears to my needs. He wants us to be genuine with Him. That is real intimacy.

Some people believe it is disrespectful to go to God with minor requests. They think He is too busy for them, and they should only ask things that are really important. They imagine God as if He doesn't want to be bothered unless it is a matter of life or death.

I believe exactly the opposite. I think it honors God when we include Him in our little, everyday concerns.

Proverbs 3:6 says, **"In all your ways acknowledge Him, and He shall direct your paths"** (NKJV).

Asking Him for little things means we are always thinking about Him and we believe nothing is too small for Him to consider.

I think that is why Jeremiah wrote, **"Ah, Lord God! Behold, You have made the heavens and the earth by Your great power and outstretched arm. There is nothing too hard for You"** (Jeremiah 32:17 NKJV).

Jesus says in Luke 12:32, **"People who don't know God and the way He works fuss over these things, but you know both God and how He works. Steep yourself in God-reality, God-initiative, God-provisions. You'll find all your everyday human concerns will be met. Don't be afraid of missing out. You're My dearest friends! The Father wants to give you the very Kingdom itself"** (MSG).

Once when I was asking Him for something, He said, *"Make it the desire of your heart so I can give it to you."* Then the Lord said, *"You have desires in your heart that you don't even know about."*

I memorized Philippians 4:6 from the The Living Bible: **"Don't worry about anything; pray about everything; tell God your needs, and don't forget to thank Him."** But the God's Word translation renders verses 6-7:

"Never worry about anything. But in every situation let God know what you need in prayers and requests while giving thanks. Then God's peace, which goes beyond anything we can imagine, will guard your thoughts and emotions through Christ Jesus."

41

When God told Randy and me to build a house, we made it the desire of our hearts. That was a desire I didn't know about until He told us.

The first thing we had to do was take out a second mortgage on the house we were living in so we had money to buy some land. We agreed that we wanted to build in the same area we were living in.

Randy made out as list of what he wanted in a property: water and sewer provided by public utilities, town trash pickup, and piped in natural gas that would not require an above ground tank. I wanted to live in town close to neighbors, have lots of trees around us, and be under a street light. As we looked around town and outside its limits, nothing worked for us.

We didn't want to live isolated out in the country or near a chicken house. After several months, we concluded that all the good undeveloped lots in town had already been sold. There was one scruffy property in town we kept returning to, but I thought it was ugly.

It was my birthday and I felt forgotten. Randy and I don't exchange gifts, so I asked God to give me a present. Suddenly that scruffy lot came to mind and I could see our house on it. I knew He was giving it to me.

We discovered it already had a sales contract on it. But God showed me it was *mine*. Our neighbor, a realtor, tried to discourage us but I asked him to put another contract on it anyway.

Randy and I marched around this lot and claimed it. We poured out a gallon of olive oil over the property lines. We knew it was ours. The other buyer could not come up with the money on time and got a 60-day extension, but we were not dissuaded. Eventually, we were able to buy it.

The bank said they were amazed that we got the lot. But I wasn't. It was the desire of my heart. The Lord told us this about prayer:

"Prayer is for you. Prayer never reveals anything to Me that I AM unaware of. Prayer is humbling yourself to ask, and letting your faith rise to receive.

"The way you live your life is very much like a prayer. When you pray about little things throughout the day, it's not a formal time of prayer, it's mindful prayer. That's the result of thinking about Me all the time and having a running dialogue. It's the communion aspect of prayer, meaning intimate fellowship."

42

Practicing our Christianity at someone else's expense.

"'Beware of the scribes... who devour widows' houses, and for a pretense make long prayers'"

(Mark 12:38, 40 NKJV).

By Randy

We were holding one of our annual "Peru dinners" in Redemption Depot, the meetinghouse behind our home. Our daughter-in-law is from Peru. Her cousin pastors a Protestant congregation there and has a gift for evangelism.

Peru is a very poor country. What we consider poverty in the United States seems middle class in comparison. This pastor lives sacrificially to help his people, so we decided to help him. Every year, Shiloh Ministries raised money for his outreach. We cooked and sold homemade chicken 'n' dumplings after church one Sunday in the Fall. It became a popular area event.

Out of this little 20- x 30-foot building, we sold hundreds of dinners in a couple hours. During the rush, three kitchens on our premises were kept busy to get meals to people who had bought tickets or just showed up.

We sold complete dinners for five dollars, including beverages and desserts. Because we priced them so inexpensively, lots of people gave donations in addition, and the events succeeded in raising many thousands of dollars each time.

One year, among those who came to volunteer was a man we knew through a mutual friend. He was getting in the way in the busy kitchen, so I was asked to take him outside and distract him so he didn't feel rejected. He was a high-maintenance person who got his feelings hurt very easily.

This man was a flagrant homosexual whom some of our visitors would have found offensive. I was really being asked to shield our guests from him. I took him to the fish pond in front and made small talk until the press of patrons subsided. We were both getting hungry, so I finally led him to Redemption Depot so we could get something to eat.

A little while later, I passed by him while I was walking one of our visitors to her car. This man was having a conversation with another visitor who was clearly uncomfortable. It almost looked like he had her pinned against her vehicle, "witnessing" to her. He was relentless as he told her about his faith.

I knew his motive was evangelism, but he was oblivious to the response of the woman he had cornered. I could see she was trying to get away from him. Her body language showed her extreme distress, but his sensitivity over getting his own feelings hurt did not extend to anyone else's..

This concerned me for her sake. By the time I finished escorting the other woman to her car, their conversation was over. Apparently the woman figured out how to escape. This was disturbing not only to her but to me. I asked the Lord to explain what I had observed, and He said, "He's practicing his Christianity at someone else's expense."

I was dumfounded. I knew his intentions were honorable, but the way he went about "witnessing" was overbearing. The Lord was showing me that we can all be guilty of this, and what a bad reflection it is on our beliefs.

I have observed this kind of behavior before. Usually it's in a public place, and the person doing the evangelizing is trying to fulfill his Christian responsibility to take the Gospel to others. In most cases, I knew these men who wanted to share about faith in Jesus, and they were sincere. But a form of pride had entered and made them more concerned about what they had to share than whether someone else could receive it from them. They were insistent to the point of being obnoxious, and insensitive to the point of being arrogant. Their efforts accomplished the opposite of what they intended.

Conversely, there are many people who follow the Christian faith, yet are unwilling to tell others about it. I remember discussing this with one man who was an executive for a large and prestigious corporation. As we talked, he told me it was immodest and disrespectful for him to tell others about his spirituality. "Undignified," I think he said.

Some folks are unsure of themselves and feel intimidated at the prospect of evangelizing. But the best way to share our faith is not in words but by our lifestyle. It should be one of joy – not mere happiness of the moment, but a jubilant and grateful response to God's eternal love for us.

The Lord told Barbara and me that joy is our spiritual weapon of choice for the times we live in. There is an absence of joy in the world, so when people see it in us, they will want to know where it comes from and how to get it. And it will be our privilege to tell them! The Lord taught us:

"Joy is a very strong anchor. It holds through storms and floods. It steadies you when the enemy causes fear to upset your boat. If you have joy, fears lose their power. Your mind doesn't see negative consequences; instead it sees all things working together for good. Joy produces peace and stability."

43

You're standing on the edge of a feather and trying to tell Me what the whole bird looks like.

"For we know in part and we prophesy in part. But when that which is perfect has come, then that which is in part will be done away" (I Corinthians 13:9-10 NKJV).

By Barbara

I did it again. While I was trying to explain to Randy what God was doing, the Lord corrected me:

"How do you know what I will do? You're standing on the edge of a feather and trying to tell Me what the whole bird looks like."

Then He added—

"It's hard to take things as they come, isn't it? That means you have no idea what will happen before they arrive, and you have absolutely no control after they get here. Total trust is required."

It reminded us of the parable of the three blind men who came across an elephant. One bumped into its leg and concluded it was a tree. Another felt its trunk and said it was a snake. The third touched its tail and declared it was a broom.

We are like the three blind men. We each know in part, according to our experience, our understanding and how observant we are. What makes us think we can figure out what God is doing? '

"'For My thoughts are not your thoughts, nor are your ways My ways,' says the Lord. 'For as the heavens are higher than the earth, so are My ways higher than your ways, and My thoughts than your thoughts'" (Isaiah 55:8-9 NKJV).

In Psalm 2, David asks, **"Why do the nations rage, and the people plot a vain thing? The kings of the earth set themselves, and the rulers take counsel together, against the Lord and against His Anointed, saying, 'Let us break Their bonds in pieces and cast away Their cords from us.'"** Then David proclaims, **"He who sits in the heavens shall laugh…"** (vss. 1-4 NKJV).

David is talking about nations which scheme against God's purposes, and rulers who conspire in opposition to the Lordship of Jesus, and refuse to receive correction. But God sees through their intentions and laughs at their feeble efforts to undermine His authority. Do you think He could be laughing at us, too, for trying to control things?

All my life, I have had a problem with controlling. I've heard that people say I am bossy. It's not that I want to dominate others, I want them to know and do what is in their best interest. The pride comes when I am convinced I know better than they do what is good for them.

When I just give advice, others think they can take it or leave it. So I'm not that gentle with them. I *tell* them what is best for them, and I can be pushy. My way is a poor demonstration when I tell people to trust the Lord.

Once, He told Randy and me:

"Trusting Me means trusting Me no matter what, or else there would be no reason to trust Me at all. If you trusted Me only for those things which were convenient and predictable, that's really justifying yourself by claiming My stamp of approval on your life.

"It's trusting Me with the things you can't predict or control and which aren't pleasant that makes a man or woman of God. That is laying down your claim to Self and taking up the cross of Christ."

He added:

"How do you keep from controlling? Let Me be in charge. When you feel responsible for the outcome of things, then you take it personally when you can't control them.

"I AM already the Lord of all Creation, but I AM not Lord of your life unless you allow Me.

"'Ought' and 'should' thinking means that you are trying to be lord and decree what's best for other people. It's hard being lord, isn't it? Wouldn't you like Me to do that for you?"

And another time He said:

"Do you really comprehend how I see you as My child? It's not a mere form of address, it's a station in My family. I look upon you and see Myself because of what I have put in you. I see My heart and I hear My words. That's why I also want My peace to dwell in you. What a joyful day it will be when you truly learn to rest in Me.

"I want you to learn to be a good steward of joy. Nurture it. Coax it to grow. Think of it as My expression in you so it equates to being like Me. Master it and it will serve you well.

"Learn to let go of controlling and you'll be free of the weight. Learn to embrace joy and you'll feel well."

44

What does a pillar do? It takes weight.

"He who overcomes, I will make him
a pillar in the temple of My God,
and he shall go out no more"
(Revelation 3:12 NKJV).

By Randy

I had an assistant who helped me write and produce the *Manna* newspaper for many years. We made it a tradition not to give each other gifts on special occasions. Instead, we exchanged Scriptures.

One Christmas, he handed me this verse: **"He who overcomes, I will make him a pillar in the temple of My God, and he shall go out no more. I will write on him the name of My God and the name of the city of My God, the New Jerusalem, which comes down out of heaven from My God. And I will write on him My new name"** (Revelation 3:12 NKJV).

At first, I didn't know what to make of it. Obviously it is intended for people who overcome adversity in the end times. But what did that have to do with me? And trying to imagine what it means to be a pillar was beyond my understanding. So later, I asked the Lord, and He responded with a question: **"What does a pillar do? It takes weight."**

The Lord can pack volumes of understanding in a brief statement. I pictured in my mind a gigantic pillar holding up God's magnificent temple. But I didn't think He was telling me I was essential to the structure of His house. So what else could it mean? As I pondered, He showed me.

Sometimes, God will put weight on us to prove a point to someone else who needs to recognize His involvement in man's daily affairs. When He does that, He knows we can bear the load, and it is a great privilege.

Early in my new life as a Christian, I read *Foxe's Book of Martyrs*, a graphic sixteenth-century account of the sacrifices and traumatic deaths of the martyrs of the early Church. As these men and women surrendered their lives for their beliefs, they were at total peace – even joyful – counting it an honor to give their all for the cause of the Gospel. Their courage in the face of horrendous persecution eventually won the hearts of the enemies of their faith, and contributed to the conversion of the Roman empire.

I read another book, *The Story of Liberty*. It is a classic account of the suffering endured by those who stood for the freedom found in knowing God. They contradicted the prevailing leadership of the institutional Church. Some of those who suffered the most had translated and published the Scriptures so God's Word could be understood and accessible to people other than the clergy.

44

The Lord was not saying He would require such a sacrifice from me. There are everyday situations in which He has put weight on me to reveal Himself to someone else.

In general, I have led a pretty trouble-free life. But in those instances when I have suffered, I knew it was part of my faithfulness to trust God conspicuously.

When I sank our station wagon in West Ocean City Harbor on the Fourth of July while I was launching our boat… When I was as good as fired from the Christian newspaper ministry I founded… When I slipped on some black ice and suffered what my surgeon called "a life-changing injury"… When a flash flood put two feet of toxic storm water on our property, ruined our ministry meetinghouse, and we had to rebuild the side of our home… When our bank essentially called in our mortgage and I thought we would lose our house… These were all occasions for panic or to demonstrate trust in God by having peace. How I handled them was my choice.

Sometimes the weight we bear is not something God puts on us, it is simply life. Jesus said, **"'In the world you will have tribulation; but be of good cheer, I have overcome the world'"** (John 16:33 NKJV). He was telling His disciples to take their eyes off their present-day circumstances and put them on spending eternity with Him.

Bearing weight, whether it is from God or the world we live in, does not have to be an unpleasant thing. Our challenge is not our circumstances but the way we respond to them. What seems in the moment like suffering may actually be the way to greater blessings. The Lord told us:

"Trials and suffering are where I perfect you. I cannot perfect you in comfort and convenience because you're not desperate for Me. But when you cling to Me for dear life, two things happen: You're willing to let Me change you, and your situation becomes a testimony of My faithfulness.

"Then you know I have used your suffering not only to perfect you but to draw others closer to Me. That was the only reason Paul and the early disciples found joy in their suffering. They were a spectacle for the sake of the Gospel, and look at how I used them. Where would you and millions of others be without their suffering?

"No man ever suffered more than Jesus, and no man was more perfect or drew more people to Me. His suffering was the greatest witness of all time, and the greatest blessing for mankind."

45

If we reflect God's character, the world will not be able to withstand us.

"Now then, we are ambassadors for Christ,
as though God were pleading through us:
We implore you on Christ's behalf,
be reconciled to God"
(II Corinthians 5:20 NKJV).

God's Sayings – *Proverbs, Enigmas & Riddles*

By Barbara

The Lord was explaining to Randy and me about the Scripture **"...you shall be holy; for I am holy...."** (Leviticus 11:44 NKJV), and He said it means that if we reflect His character, the world will not be able to withstand us.

There are many people who don't just ignore the teachings of Christianity but disdain them. Christians can spend a lot of time trying to figure out who the antichrist will be, while disregarding the antichrist spirit which is prevalent in the world today.

In my lifetime, I have seen public response to church change from being the norm for families, to being considered irrelevant. Where else will people hear about God's love? There are Christian broadcasting, books, and some accurate presentations of faith in the entertainment industry, but people need to see that faith works for those they encounter in everyday life.

God has appointed us to be His ambassadors to the world around us, and to carry His message of love to those He brings into our sphere of influence.

"Now then, we are ambassadors for Christ, as though God were pleading through us: We implore you on Christ's behalf, be reconciled to God" (II Corinthians 5:20 NKJV).

What does it mean to be an ambassador? It is more than being a government emissary to another country. An ambassador discloses no will or opinion of his own. His role is to accurately represent the wishes and policies of the one who sends him.

This is not just about us, it's about the people around us, especially those in the world who don't know God. II Peter 3:9 (NKJV) says, **"The Lord is... not willing that any should perish but that all should come to repentance."**

When Jesus gave His disciples The Great Commission, He was telling them to be ambassadors – missionaries. His followers are still missionaries, not just to foreign countries but at home.

The Lord told us what this means for the times we live in:

"The things you have read about and watched on television in the past, you will see with your own eyes and experience with your heart in times to come.

45

"The world does not know it is in a place of decision. That is why My missionaries need not to lose heart. The job of spreading the Gospel has more souls depending on it now than at any time before.

"No corner of Earth will remain unaffected. People gripped by fear will have only one hope – the light and the peace of those who know Christ. Delusions will grow stronger as your enemy the devil brings more convincing counterfeits to deceive people.

"In some countries, public institutions which once taught spiritual truth will no longer be permitted to do so. The time will come when people seeking the truth must ask Christians, and all Christians will need to see themselves as missionaries.

"It's not enough to pray that your own family be saved. Picture yourself boarding a train to Paradise while your unredeemed neighbors plead to go along, and you just wave goodbye to them. That is how selfish My people are when they do not see themselves as missionaries.

"This is the beginning of preparation. If I AM not willing that any should perish, then My people must not be willing either."

Another time, the Lord told us about the harvest that is to come:

"You've read that all Creation is groaning in anticipation of the revelation of the true sons of God. Lost souls are also groaning as they wait. You Christians think the world is resisting you. No, Satan is trying to withstand you. The world is testing you to see if you are really the true sons of God. Mere words are not proof; the world wants documentation. They want to see hearts that are living epistles, as though I Myself were pleading through you, 'Be reconciled to God.' Dare you believe such a harvest can happen on a wide scale?

"When you quote My Word about the good things I have prepared for those who love Me, do you think they all come at once, or only in designated seasons? I AM saving the best for last. Ahead is not just a season but a dispensation of grace equal to the price Jesus paid to purchase it. This will justify Jesus taking the punishment for the sin of the whole world. It will signal the time has arrived to choose whom you will serve. The season for being double-minded will end. Men will either be for Me or against Me."

46

I didn't send you there to have all the answers, I sent you there to be yourself.

"For it is God who works in you both to will and to do for His good pleasure" (Philippians 2:13 NKJV).

By Randy

I enjoyed being part of our weekly community dinners at The Son'Spot Christian Fellowship Center in Ocean City. When Barbara and I started holding them, we asked the Lord whom to invite. I pictured us going to the nearby boardwalk and trying to figure out who looked like they needed a free meal. I was surprised when the Lord responded, **"Who would I invite?"**

We knew the answer was, **"Whosoever will,"** a reference to what He said in Revelation 22:17 (KJV), **"And whosoever will, let him take the water of life freely."**

We were not supposed to look for people who appeared indigent or down and out. During the summer tourist season, a lot of teenagers come to the resort to hang out at the beach. Many of them end up homeless and sleep on couches if someone will take them in for a night. Certainly they could use a free meal.

However, the purpose of the dinners was not just to feed poor people. The Lord wanted us to bring people into The Son'Spot so they could experience His love. So everyone was invited.

Giving passersby on the boardwalk a printed pass was placing something of value in their hands, which worked much better than an oral invitation. So we photocopied hundreds of tickets, detailing the time and location on the front, and declaring on the back, "Why? Because Jesus Loves You!"

With help from volunteers and The Son'Spot staff, we organized those dinners for 12 years until we left to begin Shiloh Ministries in our home. The free meals continued. They attracted workers from the boardwalk, beach patrol lifeguards, police officers, hungry kids, and lots of homeless alcoholics.

Barbara was in charge of the kitchen. She made it a point to serve the best food possible. Spaghetti was the most popular meal that produced the least amount of wasted food. We would fix dinners to go so people could take them home for later or pick one up for a friend. Generosity reflected God's nature, which we wanted to demonstrate.

When it was people's first time at The Son'Spot, often they felt out of place in a building whose picture windows declare, "Jesus is Lord!" But as they returned each week, they got used to it. And they got used to us, too.

Slowly these street kids came to trust the dinners and the servers. The Lord had given Barbara and me instructions not to preach from the stage and make it an "us and them" encounter. I had originally envisioned it like a homeless shelter or rescue mission atmosphere, where our guests would participate in spiritual activities like singing and sharing. But the Lord specifically told us not to do that.

He said if this were really to be a free dinner, we couldn't make the people jump through our religious hoops. Someone should be able to come in, eat his meal without being disturbed, and leave with nothing being required of him. If we could do that, He said, then it would truly be free.

Since we could not preach or share testimoniess from behind a microphone, the best way to minister was to sit with out guests at the tables and eat dinner with them. So each week I asked the Lord where He wanted me to sit. When He told me, I knew He had prepared people there for the fellowship.

At first, the folks I sat with were quiet. I felt like I was doing a solo. I tried to draw them into a conversation but they did not engage. As we got to know each other and they learned to confide in me, they started asking questions. They wanted to honor us and the atmosphere of The Son'Spot, so they asked about sweeping religious concepts. Their questions were things like, "If God really loves us, why would He make a place like hell and threaten to send us there?"

These were street kids with about a 20-second attention span. I was glad to give them an answer, but I couldn't even get warmed up before I would lose them. They were polite, but they really weren't listening.

This made me feel like I was wasting my time and theirs. So at home, I asked the Lord if I should direct my efforts more productively. That's when He said something that changed my entire outlook on ministry: **"I didn't send you there to have all the answers, I sent you there to be yourself."**

These kids didn't want an intellectual discussion, they wanted to be acknowledged. They wanted my attention. That's why God had me there, to show His love and not to be a know-it-all. And that's when I stopped going to The Son'Spot to minister down to the street people, and started going to see my friends who came there.

47

If everyone did what I created them to do, the whole world would be won to Christ by now.

"The fruit of the righteous is a tree of life,
and he who wins souls is wise"
(Proverbs 11:30 NKJV).

By Barbara

When God created us, before we were ever born, He placed gifts, talents and abilities in us. These special skills are not just for our personal use, but to be dedicated back to Him for His purposes.

I enjoy making things pretty – not just my own things but those of other people too. Before I was able to buy a house, I rented many places, and I always sought to make improvements and leave them in better condition when I moved out.

That same urge to upgrade applies to improving people. I want to use my motivational gift as a giver, which also generates hospitality, to bless others as a way to reveal God's love to them. It is for their sake. What I get out of it is the satisfaction of operating in the gifting God has given me.

In addition to the gifts we were created with, each of us was also given a destiny. God's has a plan for every life.

If we all are born with gifts, why isn't everyone using them to spread the knowledge and love of God? Simple. We can use those same gifts to satisfy our own selfishness, lust and greed.

Once He told Randy and me, "I wish more people would use their gifts, resources and time – not to promote Me because there is enough of that out there and that is ineffectual – but to demonstrate My Kingdom, which requires generosity and sacrifice which come from love."

When our eyes are on the temporal things of this life and not the eternal promises of God, we become sidetracked and miss the calling God placed on us. John describes these temporal things in his first epistle: **"For all that is in the world – the lust of the flesh, the lust of the eyes, and the pride of life – is not of the Father but is of the world"** 2:16 (NKJV).

These are the same things which Satan used to tempt Jesus in the wilderness. When he asked Jesus to command stones to become bread, he was tempting Him with hunger – lust of the flesh. When he offered to give Jesus all the kingdoms on Earth, he was tempting him with lust of the eyes – greed. And when he told Jesus to throw Himself from the pinnacle of the temple because the angels would not allow Him to be harmed, he was tempting Him with the pride of life – putting God's Word to the test.

47

Satan, also called "the tempter," tempts us with the things of the world too. His intent is to distract us from the destinies God ordained for our lives.

When Randy and I were planning to be married, he never proposed to me. We both had an unspoken understanding that our lives were destined to be spent with each other. We knew God was calling us to be a team for His Kingdom. God's purpose was for us to minister together.

In our 37 years of marriage, we have spent our time and devoted our energy to what the Apostle Paul called "running the race."

It began when Randy helped with the ministry I had started with my children – puppet shows. Then we got involved with The Son'Spot Christian Fellowship Center in Ocean City, where we ended up organizing free community dinners and breakfasts for 12 years. Randy created a regional newspaper out of the donor newsletter for our area Christian radio station. It lasted for over 25 years. We pioneered Shiloh Ministries, which holds events and brings in speakers who teach on intercessory prayer and the prophetic. And we have led many prayer events all around the Chesapeake Bay. Plus we have written 12 books together.

Ministry has been our full-time job, and God has been faithful to supply our needs. We have often said, "We don't have savings accounts or a stock portfolio; we invest in the Kingdom of God because it yields the best returns."

During prayer one day, the Lord said to us, **"If everyone did what I created them to do, the whole world would be won to Christ by now."**

Imagine. If we put our eyes on the eternal instead of the temporal, He empowers us to bring in the lost, the backsliders and the prodigals. II Peter 3:9 (NKJV) says God is **"not willing that any should perish but that all should come to repentance."** He wants everyone to experience the joy of His salvation. He told us:

"The joy of your salvation is first eternal. It's gratitude that expands beyond time. It's grace that releases you from the clutches of the world. It's the promise of everlasting peace. Joy is so much more than a fire escape from hell. It is anticipation of heaven's ongoing mysteries. And it is the satisfaction of tempering your being into its destiny."

48

Pray for the land ahead of the people, for the land is more cursed than the people are.

"If My people, who are called by My name, will humble themselves and pray and seek My face and turn from their wicked ways, then I will hear from heaven, and I will forgive their sin and will heal their land" (II Chronicles 7:14 NIV).

By Randy

In Fall, 2007, the Lord directed Barbara and me to sail across the Chesapeake Bay. I was thrilled. I like boat rides.

We could accomplish this by taking a passenger ferry from the Eastern Shore of Maryland to Tangier Island, in the middle of the bay. Then we would catch a second ferry from Tangier to the opposite shore in Virginia.

Although I expected to have fun, it wasn't a pleasure cruise. The Lord had instructions for us. He wanted me declare things while we were on the ferries. "Your voice travels farther over the water than it does on land," He explained. Then He started downloading pages of Scriptures for me speak, and told me to proclaim them to the four points of the compass. They were Scriptures to bless the land, the water and the people.

I was shown that the Chesapeake Bay prophetically represents four things: government, the military, commerce and the nation's borders.

The state capitals of Delaware, Maryland and Virginia, plus Washington, D.C., are all in the vicinity of the bay. Also, the U.S. Naval Academy, Patuxent River Naval Air Station, Norfolk Navy Base, and numerous other military installations.

The Chesapeake has produced a bounty of scale fish and shellfish, and has been a thoroughfare for commercial shipping. And it empties into the Atlantic Ocean at the nation's Eastern Gate.

As the Lord prepared us for our journey, He instructed us to "take territory" for His Kingdom by anointing the soles of our shoes with oil and declaring a blessing everywhere our feet trod. Then He said, "Pray for the land ahead of the people, for the land is more cursed than the people are."

Until He said that, we understood the significance of everything He told us to do. But this concept was totally new to us, so we asked for clarification..

Scripture says the iniquities of the fathers are passed down to the third and fourth generations of their children. Where people are concerned, curses have a prescribed duration. But in II Chronicles 7:14, it appears that until the land is redeemed by repentance, it remains cursed as a result of sin.

"If My people, who are called by My name, will humble themselves and pray and seek My face and turn from their wicked ways, then I will hear from heaven, and I will forgive their sin and will heal their land" (II Chronicles 7:14 NIV).

48

Up until that time, whenever I cited II Chronicles 7:14, I didn't pay much attention to **"and will heal their land."** I thought "their land" was a reference to the people and the culture within the geographic borders of a country. As the Lord instructed us, we came to understand He was referring to terra firma, the ground itself. The Lord also showed us that the land, when cursed, holds people back from being saved.

When we sailed across the bay that Fall, we recognized that we were being called to take intercessors on a similar trip to Tangier Island, which the Lord told us is "the pearl in the oyster." He was referring to the prolific camp meetings which were held there in the early 1800s, and the spiritual heritage of the descendants of those islanders, many of whom still live on the island.

In May, 2008, we took 43 intercessors to pray with the residents of Tangier Island for the land surrounding the bay, the bay itself, and the 17 million people living around it. Afterward, the Lord told us:

"The Body of Christ needs to know that revival is not to vindicate them so they can look down on sinners. Revival is, 'Start with me so I can show the way to sinners.'

"It is My people who have to repent first. As they humble themselves and seek Me, I will awaken the land.

"While the land is cursed, it will not yield its increase. It is dormant. It is not guarding its own borders. It is not celebrating My goodness. It is not conforming to its design purpose because it is weighed down with curses from sin.

"I will awaken the land to reestablish itself. I will heal it from the stain of iniquity. And I will bring it back to its bounty. The land, when healthy, does not grudgingly produce fruit; it glories in its fertility. It was made to be productive; and when it is free from curses, it is joyful in its abundance.

"And as I do to the land, so I will do to the people. It takes those who know Me to first humble themselves and begin the process. This is repentance, which brings revival not only to men but to all Creation.

"I pronounced a blessing on the land when I formed it. Men strayed and robbed the land of its blessing. But because their words have the power of life and death, men can also cause the land to be restored by their repentance."

49

What does it profit a man if he wins the whole world to Christ and loses his own family?

"For what will it profit a man if he gains the whole world, and loses his own soul?"
(Mark 8:36 NKJV).

This part by Barbara

I was talking to a woman on the phone whom I hadn't met. By her conversation, I assumed she was single until I asked if anyone else lived with her. In a condescending tone she said yes, her husband, but he drank too much. I heard a religious spirit in the next thing she said, "but I rebuke that spirit in him all the time."

She was blaming her husband while oblivious to the fact that she was holding him in bondage. Religious spirits make us think we are doing righteously when we are actually cursing people. This cursing had settled in her liver and she had to have a portion of it removed.

The Bible says about a man and wife that the two shall become one flesh. I said she was cursing the other half of her flesh, and thus cursing herself. I told her to bless him, even write down 10 things she loved about him, and let him know them. They needed to laugh a lot together. I did not know they were going on a week's vacation for their 22nd anniversary.

As she let go of that cursing and religious spirit and began to bless her husband, I believed they would truly bond and could both finally get set free.

When we don't honor our spouses, then we are not only cursing them but ourselves. Religious spirits can cause us to sacrifice our families for what these spirits convince us is righteousnesss,

Raising my three children alone, I didn't allow them to eat candy or watch anything but Christian TV. I was very controlling. Most of that was a spirit of fear and a religious spirit. When they were grown and on their own, they rebelled against my strict parenting. They ate tons of candy and allowed their children to have as much as they wanted. Their televisions were on continuously. Now wisdom has kicked in and they no longer do that.

When they were young and I wasn't working at one of the many jobs I needed to support us, I was running all over the place ministering. We ministered together as a family, and most of it was wonderful. But I put the ministry ahead of my kids, and confused obedience with self-righteousness.

Once the Lord told me that parents with rebellious children need to repent of the pride in themselves. Self-righteousness and controlling are pride.

49

This part by Randy

I was one of those children who obediently went with my parents to church, but turned my back on their beliefs when I became old enough to make my own decisions. I did not consider spiritual matters to be relevant, and I held ridicule in my heart toward those who did.

As a young man I dabbled in Eastern Mysticism, even chanting with Nichiren Shoshu Buddists for a short time because one of my coworkers told me this was a way to obtain my material desires. But I made no commitment to it. The spiritual man in me was not yet awake.

I eventually became desperate when I saw that my life was squandered without any meaningful prospect, and I returned to the teachings of my youth. When my spirit man did wake up, I gave myself wholly to Christ, and I developed great respect for pastors and ministry leaders.

But as I pursued Christianity, I recognized a pattern among some men in ministry that concerned me. A few of these shepherds, who were to follow the example of Jesus and lay down their lives for their flocks, led very different lives at home. Their wives were given no choice when these men entered the ministry. It was as if their wives didn't count. Often, their children were insolent or rebellious. These men had sacrificed their families to the god of self-righteousness.

I asked the Lord about this, and He declared back to me a variation of a familiar Scripture:

"What does it profit a man if he wins the whole world to Christ and loses his own family? For his family is his soul."

The Gospels tell us it profits a man nothing if he gains the whole world but loses his own soul. Souls are important to God. They are the essence of who we are that survives this mortal body. That's why the Proverbs say wise is the man who wins souls.

God also places a high value on the family. It is an earthly representation of the relationship mankind is to have with Him. He once told Barbara and me:

"As the family goes, so goes the Church; as the Church goes, so goes the government."

50

Teamwork is shared vision, shared responsibility and shared workload.

"Can two walk together,
except they are agreed?"
(Amos 3:3 NKJV).

By Randy

People tell Barbara and me we make a great team.

We have one basic rule. We don't do anything unless we agree. We must be in one accord, whether it is a decision about something around the house or a ministry activity.

When I was young and imagined what it was like to be married, I wanted an equal relationship. I thought of a wife as a partner. Barbara wanted someone who would share every part of her life, someone who would be a team with her in all her projects.

We didn't start our life together that way, however. When I thought about having a partner, the one thing I didn't take into account was my own insecurity and selfishness.

I was 34 when we said our vows, and I had not been married before. I married the woman who led me to the Lord. It was like the Florence Nightingale effect in reverse – the patient fell in love with his nurse.

I was moving into Barbara's house with my two big, smelly dogs and all my junk. I was used to doing things alone, undistracted. I had no parenting skills. And I did not know how to be sensitive to the needs of a wife. Barbara had her own baggage. Life had taught her not to trust men. Our diverse backgrounds set the stage for a lot of bickering.

We fought so much that three days after we returned from the honeymoon, I called the clerk of court to see about getting our marriage annulled. He said I would need a lawyer, and I had no money for that. I concluded that I had taken a marriage vow before God, so I determined to ride it out, even when Barbara suggested divorce.

Things stayed this way for two years. When we weren't getting along, we still prayed and ministered together. Barbara kept saying that we needed to be a team. I thought, "We're married. The Bible says we're one flesh. What more does she want?"

Barbara wanted to be reassured. "Tell me you love me," she would say. "When I'm ready," I responded. I thought, in order to be sincere, I had to feel it first before I said it. Sometimes that could take awhile. I had to learn to respect her feelings and not just my own.

Some friends came to pray for us. We asked if the Lord was showing them anything. "Yes," they said, "you both have a spirit of competition."

It was true. We repented and asked the Lord to help us.

About six months later, we were working on something together and I realized it had been a long time since we'd had an argument. We traced it back to when we prayed about the spirit of competition.

As the Lord continued to teach us about our marriage, our teamwork continued to improve. Perhaps the biggest of all the lessons was what we call "The Mirror Image Principle."

I still needed to be delivered from resentment. I came under attack while we were riding in the car and Barbara – not one to put up with selfishness – got out and started walking. I eventually picked her up and we rode back in icy silence. By the time we got home, she was moving to California.

I got alone with the Lord and asked Him what happened. He responded:

"Your relationship with your wife is a mirror image of your relationship with Me. So if you're having problems, don't look at her. Look at yourself. Get your relationship right with Me and I'll take care of the woman."

He told me to stay focused in prayer and the Word. After a couple weeks, we made up and our marriage was better than ever.

I also had to learn about being double-minded. The Lord asked me, "What does My Word say about the double-minded man?" I answered from the first chapter of James, "He's like a wave tossed on the sea, unstable in all his ways, and that man should expect to receive nothing from God."

He continued, "You know I see you and Barbara as one flesh, right? That means, since you're one flesh, that whenever you disagree, you're just like the double-minded man." It was our incentive to continue pursuing more agreement and teamwork.

Then, one day, seemingly out of nowhere, the Lord told us both we were "committing emotional adultery." Neither of us was guilty of infidelity so we wondered what He meant, and asked.

"Emotional adultery is when you love the person you want your spouse to be, and not the person your spouse is."

We changed our attitude and became a team. Years afterward He told us, "Teamwork is shared vision, shared responsibility and shared workload."

Afterword

By Randy

The importance of making daily declarations out loud is not only the authority of our spoken words. This a form of ministry to ourselves. Our inner man receives and agrees with them.

The Lord gave us these declarations to use during times of prayer, not so we could inform Him of any needs we had, but to build faith as we increase our confidence and expectation.

DAILY PRAYERS

I take authority over my being and command my spirit to be in charge of me today. I direct my soul and my body to yield to my spirit. I call myself into agreement and declare I am grateful, I am teachable, and my desire is to do the will of the Spirit of the True and Living God. I call my spiritual senses to engage today. Spiritual eyes, see in the spirit. Spiritual ears, hear in the spirit. And spiritual heart, comprehend the things of the spirit.

I put on the mind of Christ which is to serve and obey. And I put on the whole armor of God. I gird my loins with the belt of truth. I put on the breastplate of righteousness. I cover my feet with the preparation of the Gospel of peace. I take up the shield of faith with which I quench all the fiery darts of the evil one. I put on the helmet of salvation. And I take up the Sword of the Spirit, the Word of the True and Living God which accomplishes what You send it forth to do, does not return to You void, and shall never pass away.

Father, I ask You today for wisdom, understanding and knowledge; discernment, discretion and diplomacy; common sense, compassion and humility; a heart broken for the lost, witty invention, felicity, patience, influence and favor.

ASSIGNING PLACES OF HONOR

I assign places of honor in my heart, in my home, in my household, on my street; and in my town, county, state, region and nation:

- to God's sovereign glory.
- to the Holy Spirit.
- to healing, deliverance and encouragement.
- to revelation and praise.
- to the love and peace of God.
- to God's government.
- to the joy of God's salvation.
- to signs, miracles and wonders.
- to prophecy, worship and forgiveness.
- to holiness, faith and repentance.

DAILY DECLARATIONS

I declare…

- I see today as an opportunity.
- I will stand fast.
- My faith shall not be moved.
- My strength is in the Lord, and He is faithful.
- My joy does not depend on other people but it comes from the Lord.
- Even my sorrows are but light afflictions which make the way for God's glory to be revealed in me.
- I see God's hand at work so my circumstances don't become my whole world.
- I know with assurance that God is in all of the situations I can think of, to produce a good outcome for everyone involved.
- I perceive that reality is not what my senses detect; reality is the unshakable truth of God's Word.
- As my faith is tested, I will grow into the measure of God's joy for me.
- God has chosen me out of the world and I belong to Him.
- I am greatly blessed, highly favored and deeply loved.
- I have God's sufficiency, power and authority.
- I choose peace today; I am a peacemaker.
- I will not give power to evil by submitting to fear.
- Joy is my compass for today and I am grateful.
- I live in the Kingdom of God, which is righteousness, peace and joy in the Holy Spirit.

KINGDOM PRAYERS

Father, I declare I am a son in Your Kingdom. I trust You to provide my needs because You have my best interest at heart.

I accept where You have me and trust where You re taking me. I want to please You with faith, and position myself for what You want to do. I need Your help to do this.

PRAYER FOR FINANCES

I take authority over my finances and declare I have entered my season of increase, restoration, redemption, restitution and abundance, and I ask You, Father, to continue bringing it to pass.

I claim the resources for my assignment and pray for my stewardship skills and the unhindered supply of heaven to be released to me for all my needs.

PRAYER FOR FAMILY

Father, I commend myself and all my family members to Your grace and authority, and ask You to…

- perfect us as saints.
- instill in us Your attributes.
- enlarge our capacities for faith.
- make us productive fruitbearers for your Spirit.
- rest Your peace in us so our eyes will always be on You.
- teach us the joy of Your salvation.
- and heal us.

I pray my day be even, not letting extremes weary or stress me but letting peace guide me today. I am not under control of my circumstances but take authority over the most challenging situations. Help me let joy infiltrate my heart, peace dictate my thoughts, and love craft my words.

I pray for peace in our family relationships, peace with our neighbors, peace in our household, and peace in our finances.

PRAYER FOR MINISTRY

Father, I have a message I know will set people free. I have insight and experience they will relate to. I don't want to keep my light to myself. Raise me up. Send me out. Make the way. And give me favor, and I will trust You to provide my needs.

PROTECTION FROM DARKNESS

Father, I pray for have my name, the names of all my family members, our properties, what we're doing, every aspect of who we are – spirit, soul, body and all tracking avenues – removed from hell and the realm of darkness. The blood of Jesus annuls all covenants with death and darkness, and His blood covers us.

In the name of Jesus, I countermand all assaults and curses from hell against me and my family members, and I raise up and establish intractable beachheads of healing for each one of us.

PRAYER FOR THE PRESIDENT AND THE NATION

Father, I pray that You send Your angels to surround our President and Vice-President and their families, and keep them safe physically, spiritually and emotionally. Establish a barrier around them to deflect all curses and witchcraft sent against them.

I pray that our President possess grace and wisdom, and have divine encounters with Your glory. Cause him to lead us into righteousness and liberty. I pray that he will mature in his faith and have the humility to consult You over every decision and every policy.

Cause our President to bring godly transformation to our government, our economy and our foreign relations, and to have wise advisors who give him godly counsel.

Father, I pray for our nation to know it is accountable to You, and to fear You. I pray that we will honor and pray for the President, his office and his Administration, with the Church setting the example. And I pray that we repent for backbiting, accusations and ungodly judgments against our leaders.